Marx at the Millennium

MARX AT THE MILLENNIUM

CYRIL SMITH

Pluto Press
LONDON • CHICAGO, IL.

First published 1996 by Pluto Press
345 Archway Road, London N6 5AA
and 1436 West Randolph
Chicago, Illinois 60607, USA

British Library Cataloguing in Publication Data
A catalogue record for this book is available from the British Library

ISBN 0 7453 1001 X hbk

Library of Congress Cataloging in Publication Data
Smith, Cyril. 1929–
   Marx at the millennium / Cyril Smith.
   183p. 22cm.
   Includes bibliographical references and index.
   ISBN 0–7453–1001–X (hbk.)
   1. Marx, Karl. 1818–1883. 2. Communism—History. 3. Socialism—
History. I. Title.
HX39.5.S559   1996
335.4—dc20   95–52759
                                                         CIP

Designed and produced for Pluto Press by
Chase Production Services, Chipping Norton, OX7 5QR
Typeset from disk by Stanford DTP Services, Milton Keynes
Printed in the EC by WSOY, Finland

DEDICATION

To my daughters, Laura and Emma. When you were babies, you began to educate me about what it meant to be a human being.

Chambers English Dictionary:

millennium *mil-en'-iem, n.* a thousand years: a thousandth anniversary: the thousand years after the second coming of Christ: (usu. *ironical*) a coming golden age.

Contents

Preface

I suppose you could say it has taken me about 50 years to write this book. I certainly didn't know I had begun when I started to think about socialism as a schoolboy in a strongly Labour household at the end of the Second World War. The election of the 1945 Labour government seemed to promise a new world, but I soon became disillusioned with the sordid compromises of the Attlee administration, so clearly betraying the hopes of millions of its supporters.

So I started to read the works of Marx and, after arriving at University College, London in 1947, I began to attend meetings of the Communist Party. Here, at last, was a systematic way to understand the world. However, this was at the time of the Cominform attack on Tito, and the Biometry Department, led by J.B.S. Haldane, was in an uproar about the Lysenko Affair. I began dimly to realise that Stalin's followers might not be telling the truth, either to me or to themselves.

Then it became obvious that they were lying their heads off, especially about the history of the Russian Revolution, the fate of its leaders and the nature of life in the USSR. I turned with excitement to the works of Leon Trotsky, and learned something about his struggle to continue the work begun in 1917. Now here, I thought, was the real theory of socialism, completely worked out. All we had to do was to 'put it into practice'.

Leon Trotsky, I learned, was the most important of those who fought against Stalin's betrayal of the Revolution. He condemned the idea that, just because its industry was state-owned, Stalin's Russia was socialist. In the struggle which eventually cost him his life, he demonstrated that the brutality, corruption and lies of the Soviet state apparatus were in direct opposition to the transition to socialism. In any case, socialism was not possible in a single country.

He never ceased to believe in the theoretical foundations of the Communist International in its early, Leninist days. This led him to predict a future trajectory for the USSR which was not borne out after the Second World War. We Trotskyists thought we could fit the developments of that time into the theoretical framework of Trotsky's struggle, that is, of the outlook of the Communist International. We reprinted his works and tried as hard as we could to propound his ideas in the changed post-war world. I thought that this outlook represented the fundamental conceptions worked out by Karl Marx, what we knew as 'scientific socialism'.

Looking back at many decades of this work, I think it was by no means the worst way to proceed, however grotesque some of our ideas and actions may look today. But in 1995 it is worse than useless to go on patching up the old notions. The events of the past few years have seen the world change so much, and contradict our picture of it so profoundly, that something much more drastic is required.

In the main, Marxists responded in one of two ways to the sequence of events which led to the collapse of the Soviet Union and its satellite states. Some heard the report that 'Marxism is dead', accepted the news as reliable, and just gave up. Others carried on as if nothing had happened, or pretended that it was all precisely what they expected.

I don't know which of these two attitudes is more in tune with the cynicism and corruption of the 1990s: either to maintain with heroic dogmatism that anything we once said must be true, simply because we once said it; or to throw away the entire work of the 'Marxist' tradition as simply a delusion. Each of these approaches — and they actually have a great deal in common — is a dishonest evasion of the real problems of our time. Instead, I think, those of us who adhered to one or other version of the 'Marxist' tradition are now obliged to re-examine the entire history of the fight for socialism and the body of 'theory' that grew out of it.

This task must be undertaken with scrupulous objectivity and with the greatest respect. Men and women like Lenin, Trotsky and Rosa Luxemburg, and millions of working people who followed them, battled for a way out of the brutal mess which is bourgeois society in the twentieth century. They refused to believe that the world of capitalism could possibly be worthy of our human nature. They devoted their lives to finding the road to a better form of society. They tried with all their intellectual powers to comprehend their own revolutionary activity within a systematic framework.

This history of struggle is of lasting value. But if you want to preserve that value, the system of ideas which is its legacy has to be subjected to rigorous criticism. Otherwise, you insult the founders of Marxism, turning their work into Holy Scripture. What is needed is a careful re-examination of the entire body of 'Marxist' doctrine, opening up all the notions which we used to assume were incontestable and asking questions which we believed were unaskable.

This process is painful, involving serious restructuring of the inside of one's head. But, after all these decades, I have been driven unwillingly to the conclusion that this thoroughgoing reassessment of the work of Karl Marx must now be undertaken. I don't believe that other people who talk about this have gone nearly far enough.

Some readers might think that in the course of these pages I have exaggerated the gulf between the ideas of Marx and the body of doctrine called 'Marxism'. If so, please excuse me, but I am convinced that it would have been a far more serious error to understate this gap.

As I reread the works of Marx over the past few years, it came as a shock to discover just how far his insights had been distorted. But then it began to dawn on me that keeping Marx and 'Marxism' quite separate from each other provided the chance to see the world more clearly. It was a world which had altered dramatically from the days when the categories of 'Marxism' seemed to be able to illuminate all problems. If Marx can be disentangled from the 'Marxist' doctrine, I believe his insights into the problems of his time become startlingly relevant to those of our own.

Even in the 1960s, when I used to talk to audiences of workers and students about *Capital*, I recall feeling that I was not being strictly 'orthodox'. I had read the *Paris Manuscripts* of 1844 when an English translation appeared in 1959, and it was obvious that their author was no 'Marxist'; but then, I told myself, he was a young man when he wrote them. However, in 1973, the publication of *Grundrisse* shook me far more deeply: Marx was forty years old when he wrote this work. I produced an essay,[1] which tried uneasily to give a 'dialectical materialist' account of what I had found in this amazing work.

In my lectures in the 1970s, I was obliged to turn more and more towards the understanding that *Capital* was about neither 'Marx's economics', nor 'capitalism'. Whatever else it included, it was chiefly about communism, a truly human society. At the end of that decade, I dropped out of political activity. In the early 1980s, almost my only involvement was to help to edit a volume containing an English translation of Marx's work on mathematics. I thought this was far enough from real life to escape the doubts which assailed me. I was wrong!

The Trotskyist group to which I had belonged for three decades exploded in 1985, as did so many apparently disparate groups on the Left around that time. I returned to the fray, determined to find out what I had been doing for over half of my life. In 1987, I wrote a little booklet[2] which – only scraping the surface – tried to look at the problems which faced 'Marxist orthodoxy'.

Although I was only too conscious of the weaknesses of this work, I imagined that it would at least begin a discussion on the Left. Wrong again! To my astonishment and dismay, people I had worked with for twenty or thirty years stopped talking to me. They were intent on 'reconstructing' the movement on its old theoretical basis, and the noise of my digging only interrupted this activity. Although I was personally upset about this, it showed me that I had to dig much, much deeper. Rereading works of Marx which I thought I knew well, I found that I didn't know them at all.

There is a responsibility for transmitting the insights of Karl Marx to a new generation who will desperately need them. This does not mean that I believe he is always 'correct', or invariably consistent. I am not trying to rediscover a god-like, infallible and all-knowing Marx. Some of the huge volume of his writings is of historical interest at most, and some of his statements are simply wrong. Even when his most important discoveries are properly understood, they will be seen to be, not ready-made answers to our problems, but pointers to a better way to pose the questions. I shall try to show how, when looked at this way, they get to the heart of precisely those problems which face the world at the end of this century.

The book proceeds thus. Chapter 1 is a brief sketch of the world today, showing what a mess it is in. This may be pretty obvious, but what is more interesting is that everybody seems to find it inconceivable that there can be any other way to live. Why should that be?

I believe that, if we can find out what Marx was trying to do, he will help us to find a way forward. However, first, the heap of ideological rubble which has been dumped on top of Marx's ideas must be excavated. In Chapter 2, I have traced the way that the 'official', 'orthodox' story of 'Marxism' arose to obscure the view of Marx.

The topmost layer, the Stalinist caricature, is easily disposed of. But it erected its falsifications on the basis of a body of doctrine which had already distorted the essence of Marx's work. This was largely the product of Karl Kautsky and Georgi Plekhanov, the theoretical leaders of the international workers' movement before 1914, and it was accepted by those who formed the Third International. (I refuse to go along with the common allegation that the process of falsification of Marx was mainly due to Frederick Engels, whatever his weaknesses.)

After this, I begin to look at what Marx's relevance for our time might be. Chapter 3 tries to show that Marx's work was primarily concerned with grasping the nature of human beings, and the way that present-day society is alien to that nature.

In Chapter 4, I contrast Marx's approach to humanity with the way that academic studies like philosophy, economics, sociology and the natural sciences investigate it. Marx, I believe, showed how each of these disciplines, in attempting to describe what humans are, both expresses and obscures their alienated life.

As an appendix to Chapter 4, I have included an article called 'Science and Humanity – Hegel, Marx and Dialectic'. This first appeared in *Common Sense*, Journal of the Edinburgh Conference of Socialist Economists, Number 15, April 1994, and I am grateful to the editors for permission to reproduce it.

In Chapter 5, I try to show how these ideas of Marx, freed from their 'Marxist' wrappings, can be brought to bear on some of the problems of the present time. It would be presumptuous to pretend to provide 'answers' to these problems. This is not only because I don't know the answers, but also because that is not what Marx's work is about. Instead, I think it attempts something more important: to clarify some of the questions which humanity will not be able to evade in the coming century. Any reader who yearns for a more prescriptive conclusion is invited to provide one.

I wish that at this point I could express my gratitude to old comrades in the Trotskyist movement for the help they have given me in the course of this work. Alas, I can't. When they found out what I was up to, most of them stopped communicating with me, because I made them feel uncomfortable. Some exceptions must be mentioned, however. Tom Kemp disagreed with some of my conclusions, but continued to discuss them with me and to give me help and encouragement until his recent death. Geoff Barr has also commented helpfully on some earlier versions of sections of this work. Many discussions with Shiraz Kassam are reflected throughout these pages, but especially in Chapter 1.

Other people, coming from quite different directions, were very helpful. Don Cuckson, whom I first got to know when he was a member of the Communist Party and I was a fervent Trotskyist, has helped me a great deal. He is engaged in a similar voyage of exploration of his own past theoretical notions. Piero Pinzauti, who will dislike a large part of what I have written, nonetheless initiated some of the impulse to write it. His Florentine vehemence helped to jolt me out of the philosophical rut in which I was stuck.

Hayo Krombach, whose Hegelian views separate him widely from my standpoint, has given me invaluable assistance on the basis of his deep knowledge of Hegel's work. Many hours of discussion with Ute Bublitz, whose own point of view will, I hope, shortly be published, have played an essential part in shaping my attitude to Marx's ideas and their relationship with those of Hegel.

Comments and criticisms of drafts of the book by Ute Bublitz, Don Cuckson, Tony Madgwick, Felix Pirani, Ben Rudder and Towfik Shomar have been invaluable. I am sorry that I have not always been able to do what they wanted me to.

When I say that none of these people can be held responsible for the many deficiencies in this book, I am doing more than offer the usual formal disclaimer. In fact, each of them disagrees with some of what I have to say, and many of the ideas have emerged only in the course of sharp disagreements with them.

I am grateful to them all.

Cyril Smith
January 1995

1 The Way We Live Now

Finally, there came a time when everything that men had considered as inalienable became an object of exchange, of traffic and could be alienated. This is the time when the very things which till then had been communicated, but never exchanged; given, but never sold; acquired, but never bought – virtue, love, conviction, knowledge, conscience, etc. – when everything, in short, passed into commerce. It is the time of general corruption, of universal venality, or, to speak in terms of political economy, the time when everything, moral or physical, having become a marketable value, is brought to the market to be assessed at its truest value.

Karl Marx[1]

Twentieth-Century Paradox

At the end of the twentieth century, humankind is not a pleasant sight. We humans have had centuries of ever-accelerating natural-scientific and technological progress. With this immeasurable advance in our ability to understand and transform the natural world, it ought to be easy to make ourselves reasonably comfortable.

Instead, humanity seems to be in the grip of some invisible, malevolent force. This uncontrollable demon impels us to tear our world apart, turning our own human productive powers against ourselves, transforming them into forces of self-destruction. Set against one another, we are reduced to a state of utter powerlessness, mere spectators of our own actions, able neither to control nor to comprehend them. This is what makes the recent changes in the world appear so strange to us.

For reasons we are quite unable to explain, we devote a huge part of our energy and ingenuity to lying and cheating, to hurting or killing each other. Over many decades, a major part of scientific and industrial activity has been devoted to fabricating the means to kill, torture and maim human beings. They functioned with great efficiency: millions perished miserably in world wars and death camps. After the Holocaust

1

and the atomic bomb had shown us just how effective we were, the third quarter of this century was overshadowed by the possibility of nuclear self-destruction bringing the whole show to a grand finale.

During the 1980s, the immediacy of the threat seemed to recede. As if a signal had been given, a dozen 'minor' paroxysms of murder erupted. Nuclear weapons, once the prerogative of the super-powers, are now 'democratically' spread around the globe. While modern means to process and transmit information knit every aspect of world economic life into ever-closer global union, brutal conflicts explode between national and religious groups, equipped by arms dealers with the latest killing machines. The outbreak of bestial savagery in the former Yugoslavia, one of the better-publicised examples, seems to point the way for the rest of the globe.

After the Second World War, a few decades of industrial expansion brought a new menace to the fore. It began to seem possible that, even without the opportunity of war, the use of modern technology would destroy the natural environment on which all human life depends. Again, this threat to humankind is both the outcome of human activity and totally out of human control.

In every part of the world, there has been a drive to expand industry and to apply the discoveries of chemistry and biology to agriculture and to medicine. The consequences, however, have never been what was intended. They include the destruction, not only of natural ecological systems, but also of older forms of social life.

Almost the whole planet is now covered by a uniform cultural sludge. It is mechanised with the latest technology, impoverished and fragmented, obsessed with surface, form, image, packaging. Appropriately, a high-tech, tabloid, 'entertainment' industry, completely motivated by the drive for profit, churns out a highly polished and debased product for the masses of every continent.

The presentation of 'news' now forms an inseparable part of this round-the-clock stream of images. Pictures of war and of natural disaster are smoothly and expertly mixed with titillating gossip and mechanically performed 'comedy'. Parallel with this, and equally obsessed with money, cultural products for a narrow middle-class layer are increasingly reduced to superficial, self-conscious posing.

Of course, millions of people try to lead decent lives amidst all this confusion, bringing up their children in the best way they can, but such remnants of humanity are pushed into the background of social life. Every day another bit disappears, as the last vestiges of communal life are replaced by the impersonal machines of state bureaucracy and the market.

This is a world which becomes less and less comprehensible to its inhabitants. To speak of the prevalence of 'selfishness' is misleading, for people now not only fail to recognise each other, but can't even recognise themselves. (Applicants for many high-powered jobs nowadays find they need 'interpersonal skills'. The ability to get on with other people needs special training it seems.)

Is it any wonder that drug abuse and alcoholism are so rife? These self-destructive responses are only futile attempts to blot out the meaninglessness and irrationality of the modern world. At a time when entire national states disintegrate, it is not surprising that over a quarter of the citizens of many countries undergo some form of treatment for mental disorder at some time in their lives.

Now, all of this is obvious to anybody who thinks seriously about it. Many will agree that this loss of control over our lives is connected with the social order sometimes known as 'capitalism'. There is much talk of the 'money-culture' and its consequences. But what is remarkable about the 1990s is that, amidst all these obvious examples of self-destruction, it has now become almost unthinkable that we might possibly live in any other way, or even that we should try.

What can explain this strange paradox? In the 1950s and 1960s, we were often told that, in the advanced countries at any rate, an adequate material standard of living had been provided for all. With the aid of the new technology, a bit more tinkering with state intervention in the economy, a little improvement in state welfare schemes, and just a few steps further down the road of decolonisation, and the year 2000 would see the solution to many of the world's problems. Now, only a politician at election time would even suggest such things – and only a fool would believe him.

For over a century, millions of people, organised in a powerful working-class movement, challenged the existing order, convinced that they were on the verge of a drastic change. A socialist future would guarantee the rational use of human creativity and resources.

In the years immediately following the Russian Revolution, this future seemed to many to be almost at hand. But the dream faded. Bottled up within a devastated, backward country, the revolution rapidly degenerated. A bureaucratised state machine, drawn increasingly into the world market, reproduced the most corrupt and brutal features of the decaying world order it claimed to replace. Even on those later occasions where despair drove masses of people into revolutionary action, they never seemed to look beyond a change of political regime and higher living standards.

When the Soviet Union broke up, and its former satellite states collapsed, there was a lot of talk about 'the end of socialism', or 'the collapse of Marxism', even 'the end of history', and that is certainly the way many people still think of it. But, long before this, the realities of Stalinism had convinced large numbers of people that bureaucratic control – this was the generally accepted meaning given to the words 'socialism' or 'communism' – was the only alternative to the power of capital. When the East European regimes collapsed, millions of working people were glad to be rid of them.

The new regimes which have appeared in the lands of the former USSR and its satellites, combine some of the monstrous remains of the old bureaucratic structures with the repulsive features of the bourgeois world. And yet, three-quarters of a century after the October Revolution, the belief is widespread that, however bestial its forms of appearance, the existing social order is the only one possible.

Even before the collapse of the Soviet bloc, the international labour movement, the only force which could challenge the power of capital, was on the retreat. During the 1980s, trade unionism shrank in size and influence in every one of the older industrial nations. While the relocation of industry to newly industrialised countries led to the emergence of a new trade unionism, it is significant that, in both old and new movements, the idea of socialism is rarely talked about.

I have pointed to some features of the world at the end of this century – that people have no control over their own lives, that they are unable to comprehend the consequences of their own actions, that social life is fragmented – and to the widespread belief that no other way of life is possible. These changes in world society, which have come upon us so rapidly, seem to form a web of corruption and inhumanity. But what is the connection between them? How can we grasp them as a unity?

The Economics of Insanity (and vice-versa)

Advances in the natural sciences, and their technological application, underlie all the changes in the way we live. During the second half of the century, humankind has put its stamp on the globe to an extent no-one could have envisaged, even a few decades ago.

Electronics has expanded into every corner of industrial and domestic life. Transport and communication have become faster and simpler, until Tokyo is next door to New York and Australasia is a part of Greater London. Medicine has made enormous strides, and is intricately involved not only with biochemistry, but with physics and even engineering. Machines are computer-controlled and factories are run by robots. The processes of life are now the basis for powerful 'biotechnological' processes in industry and agriculture. From the tiniest sub-atomic particle to the expanses of outer space, the whole universe now seems to be under reconstruction by technology, including even our own bodies.

Yet these powerful developments of human creativity are turned into something quite different by the social forms within which they are organised. As everybody knows, the most important advances in knowledge, and the most powerful applications they bring into being, are directed to mass murder and mass destruction. These now include horrific chemical and biological weapons. More 'peaceful' applications of science, directed solely towards the accumulation of immense agglomerations of wealth, have arisen largely as 'spin-offs' of the weapons industry.

Technical advance today is so fast, and on such a huge scale, that it brings with it the danger of uncontrolled and unforeseen alterations to the planet, to its chemical composition and to the interconnected structure of its biological make-up. What does this imply for the way we live, and the way we try to understand our world?

The mode in which society organises its productive activity masks the speed and extent of these changes. While the steam-engine took about 150 years to run its course, new developments in computing machinery find their expression in widely available products within a couple of years. However you measure the productive power of labour, the past twenty years have seen the potential ability to satisfy human needs take several leaps forward. In many industries and branches of agriculture, the productivity of labour has multiplied five or ten times.

What are the consequences of this forward movement? Nobody can tell. Greater ability to produce wealth must have some connection with the ability of humans to satisfy their human needs, but it is impossible to say what it is. For who knows what these needs really are?

The steady rise in the level of unemployment, whether the economy is in 'recession' or 'recovery', is only one way that the ability to produce wealth faster turns into a threat to the well-being of the producers. In the main industrial countries, the proportion of people employed in making things which people need went down steadily right through the 'boom' decades.

In the UK, for example, over seven million people worked in manu-facturing industry in 1980. By 1990 there were five million. The fall to a little over four million during the next three 'recession' years was hardly more precipitous. In the US, the proportion of the labour force in manufacturing is now around 12 per cent, and still falling.

All these changes operate on a global level. Each advance in production methods rapidly affects every part of the world, but it does so with ever-increasing unevenness. The new technology simultaneously integrates production into a world-wide undertaking and disintegrates it. What seems to benefit some people in some places appears as a disaster to others.

The steady growth of persistent long-term unemployment is closely related to the relocation of industry to areas of cheap labour, the newly industrialised countries. Meanwhile, masses of workers migrate in the opposite direction in search of higher living-standards and greater job-security. Both movements are facilitated and driven by the new technology.

Many millions of the better-off sections of the population have nothing to do with creating anything useful at all. Instead, they devote their skill and effort to other purposes, for example, persuading people to buy things they would otherwise not have thought they needed. In a world where brand names and packaging count for much more than the actual utility of goods, the media earn vast amounts of money by employing the very latest technology to spread misinformation and illusion.

Looked at on a global scale, the rise in productivity is accompanied by a widening of the gap between rich and poor countries. But even in the industrialised countries, the enhancement of the productive power of labour, instead of lightening the burden of human toil, throws some sections of the population into poverty and misery and makes others work longer and under still worse conditions. Long-term unemployment is accompanied by a rapid increase in part-time working, mainly of women and young people, the sections of society which get the worst of every shift in the economy.

Society is increasingly divided into strata whose ways of life diverge more and more widely. Those at the bottom are deprived of decent housing, education and health care. In turn, this condemns them to a life of unemployment or of the most degrading work.

Some groups seemed to have done well out of these economic changes, although the recession brought some of them down to earth with a bang. A new middle class has been able to improve its standard of living, in material terms, and so have some sections of manual workers. Many are relieved of heavy physical labour and some are provided with considerable material wealth. Actually, their very life, incorporated into the computerised system, ought to be called impoverished, at a deeper, spiritual level. For, apart from getting money, they are unable to say just what their life activity is for.

The market, of course, is what links the whole world together. Money really makes the world go round, determining every aspect of the life of society as a whole as well as the lives of individuals. But is this really the old form of exchange? Is money that convenient 'medium of exchange' described in textbooks of economics? Or rather, in the era of the transnational corporation, is it not finance which controls the rest of economic, political and social life? From politics to football, from music to newspapers, every activity is driven by the thirst for money, which does its own thing, almost as an independent force.

After the Second World War, US dominion over the globe was expressed through the strength of the dollar, and all international trade took place through its auspices. This was the financial set-up under which an unprecedented industrial expansion of production took place. Under the banner of John Maynard Keynes, governments, together with international agencies like the International Monetary Fund, thought they had the system under control.

In the late 1960s, the boom began to falter. With the Vietnam defeat, the emergence of Japan as a major economic power and the oil shocks of the 1970s, the dominance of the US dollar was severely eroded. A mountain of debt overshadowed the globe. For many decades – perhaps since the slump of the 1930s – money has been *credit-money*, whose supply could expand or contract to fulfil the requirements of the world markets. In the earlier period, central banks kept an eye on the process, adjusting the rate of interest and keeping the other banks in line.

By the end of the 1980s, all this had changed. No longer could anyone pretend that the world economy was controllable by banks, by governments or by anybody else. In 1979–81, the dominant influence of Lord Keynes just seemed to fade away. Now, instead of governments controlling the economy, the movement of debt came to control governments. Banks, central and private, counted for less as independent decision-makers, elbowed aside by new kinds of financial institution. While computers linked the world into a high-speed globalised economy, the whole thing zoomed along with nobody at the steering wheel – in fact, there wasn't any steering-wheel!

Once upon a time, it was easy to become a millionaire – at least, it was easy to understand how it could be done! You just had to employ other people to make things, which you could then sell at a profit. Banks lent you money to begin and took a part of the loot in return in the form of interest. But in this brave new world, making money from money is an end in itself, far more important than the making of goods. Of course, at no time could you get rich except at the expense of those who were poor, but now the process was in the open.

In this 'casino capitalism', the trick was not to lend money when you had too much of it, but to lend money when you didn't have any. Manufacturing and other firms raised their capital through the issue of securities, which were then bought and sold on the market for whatever people thought they were worth, or might be at some later date.

Financial wizards issued 'junk bonds', using the money invested to take over firms and merge them, then paying the investors out of profits made from the resulting rise in share prices. Others gambled on the future prices of commodities, or even of stock-market assets. In other words, *debt* was not only bought and sold, but made the subject of *betting*. And, piling madness on madness, debts were fashioned into huge pyramidal structures, ownership of each chunk of debt serving as collateral to borrow still more.

Of course, in the end it is the labour of people in factories and fields which is the source of these masses of wealth. But the predominant sections of capital are no longer those involved in manufacture or in the extraction of raw materials. Economic and social life in the older industrial countries was transformed by the decline of large-scale manufacturing industry. When the first billionaires appeared, many of them turned out to be engaged either in retailing or in the manipulation of debt.

The movement of masses of speculative money now came to determine the fate of national economies. The prosperity of these modern capitalists is not bound up with stability at all. What they like is 'volatility', unpredictability, uncontrollability. In the old days, unvarying rates of exchange between different currencies was the ideal. Today, thousands of billions of dollars change hands each day, making immense profits from fluctuations in exchange rates. The foreign exchange market is now a major source of profit for all owners of capital.

Huge amounts of wealth are 'earned' by those who manage the flotation of new firms, or the merging of existing ones. 'Consultancy', which sometimes means no more than introducing businessmen to each other, or to politicians, can yield tremendous incomes.

In the past, it might have made sense to refer to such ways of making money as 'parasitic' on the old-fashioned industrial capitalism. However, in the 1970s and 1980s, the parasites came to rule the world. Decisions about whether and where to produce can only be taken relative to the rate of interest, and to the profits which might be yielded if you closed the whole thing down and put your money into some financial speculation. Thus the power of finance is not merely independent of productive activity: it is actually destructive of it.

Inseparable from all economic changes during the past twenty years are the changed relationships between the economy and the state. In earlier times, the state was supposed to keep the masses in order, to see fair play between the owners of capital of a particular nation, and to represent them against other states. In the Keynesian era, the state entered more directly into economic life, and the state budget made up a sizeable part of national income in many countries. The state was supposed to *plan* economic development, steering it by adjusting the knobs of taxation and interest rates.

But now, all that has gone. Economic policy has to pander to the requirements of finance, rather than governing it. The chief economic function of the state is now to guarantee the health of the financial corporations, those precariously balanced edifices of debt. To complete the circle, government expenditure on such operations must, of course, be financed by borrowing yet more from these same institutions. Effectively, the state, with its central bank, is no longer the sole creator of money. The 'supply' of money issues uncontrollably from a hundred financial orifices.

The 1980s saw a violent shift from state control to deregulation and privatisation all over the world. This was inevitable, in view of the conflicting interests of national states and transnational enterprises, and the ease with which masses of speculative funds moved at the speed of light from place to place. The consequences of privatisation for many sectors of social life which had previously been taken care of by the state, like health and education, has been disastrous. Privatisation in no way meant that individuals had greater control over their lives. On the contrary, it was bound up with the mushrooming of huge, uncontrolled bureaucratic structures.

A major sequence of state scandals has revealed that bribery and corruption at the very highest level of state agencies play a major part in the globalised economy. We are not here talking about the odd 'backhander', or unfortunate anomalies, in which a few villains are found from time to time breaking the law and stealing the wealth of their fellow citizens. As scandals in Italy, Spain and Japan have illustrated, bribery, involving massive sums of money, has become a leading feature of world economic and political life. Without it, the system could not function.

The collapse of the Soviet Union and its satellites in Eastern Europe, what used to be called 'the centrally planned economies' (in the light of our increased knowledge of them, this name seems not quite as appropriate as we once thought), was closely related to these changes. The subsequent upheavals have thrown much light on the nature of modern political life.

As the market has been 'set free' to determine the lives of the inhabitants of these countries, all of the symptoms of this 'freedom' have shown themselves. Mafia-type gangs control large parts of the distribution of goods. Drug trafficking, pornography and prostitution thrive, alongside mass unemployment and hunger. Meanwhile, men and women who, quite recently, would have called themselves communists, hurry to get very rich, sometimes as agents of the transnational corporations.

The end of the Cold War was supposed to release everybody from the burden of arms production. When the time came to collect the 'peace dividend', it was found that a number of hot wars needed still more equipment. As yet, nuclear weapons have not been employed in these conflicts. But there are now some sixteen countries with atomic weapons programmes. Many more are geared up for chemical and biological armaments, and even more are now buying each new generation of 'smart' weapons.

Indeed, the trade in armaments is one of the chief factors linking the various parts of the global economy. The many armed conflicts actually killing people at this time ensure that large sums of money are accumulated by those engaged in this trade. It turns out that for many years several governments, including the US, the UK and France, had been encouraging or allowing some of their citizens to supply the very latest killing-machines to the most oppressive regimes. To be fair, often in contravention of their own laws, they sell war material to their enemies as well.

Like the lucrative trade in high-tech weaponry, the manufacture and distribution of illegal drugs had become entwined inextricably with the world banking system. Together, these two occupations now make up a sizeable portion of global commercial life. The breakdown of barriers between the Western and East European banks now gives the drug-dealers more scope to move their profits around the world. To an unknown extent, forces within the state itself participate in such dealings. Billions of 'narco-dollars' yield big profits to some of the most 'respectable' financial institutions. If these billions were to disappear, the entire system would be in trouble.

The nature of the new world is clearly revealed in the former colonial and semi-colonial countries. The disappearance of the old colonial empires was a major feature of the post-war world. The chief beneficiaries, however, were often drawn from a narrow layer of politicians and army officers. These people, sometimes dressing themselves in the most radical political clothes, fitted in well with the new financial atmosphere of the 1980s.

The concept of a 'Third World' – never a clear one – is now quite misleading. The group of former colonial and semi-colonial countries, where industrial and social development had been held back by imperialist domination, has broken into pieces. In Asia, several countries have undergone considerable economic growth, largely under the influence of the rise of the Japanese economy. Although living standards still lag far behind Europe and the US, they must now be classed as industrialised nations.

Meanwhile, many countries in Africa and Latin America have fallen still further behind. The world shortage of food which could be seen a decade or so back has been reduced in size. And yet starvation in many parts of the world, especially on the African continent, is far worse, sometimes caused by one of the many civil wars raging since the Old Order fell apart. Altogether, about one and a quarter billion men, women and children are living below subsistence levels, and the number is rising fast.

People sometimes used to refer to the older industrialised countries as 'metropolitan'. This is now a misnomer, for several of the largest cities in the world are to be found in the southern hemisphere. In 1950, the Third World comprised about two-thirds of the world's population, but only a small proportion of them lived in the ten cities which then held a million or more inhabitants. By 1990 there were 171 such cities, over 30 with more than 5 million and 9 with over 10 million. By the year 2000, it is estimated 45 per cent of the population of these countries will live in towns.

In the mega-cities which mushroomed almost overnight, millions live in shanty towns and barrios under the most miserable conditions imaginable. On every continent, the march of progress has engendered monstrous urban conglomerations, vast pools of human misery. Within sight of the most up-to-date airports, in close proximity to glass and concrete structures housing international banks, starvation is an everyday occurrence. Protecting their property against those without any is a major preoccupation of the wealthier citizens.

For a few of their inhabitants, life in these new cities mimics aspects of life in the older industrialised countries. On the other hand, every metropolis in what are still called the 'advanced' countries, has its own 'Third World'. I mean the 'cardboard city' where the homeless struggle to survive, on the margins of urban civilisation.

What unifies the items on this list of features of the new world set-up? Bewilderment, despair, self-destruction, powerlessness, disintegration, fragmentation, chaos: these are some of the words which come to mind. Many people, in various parts of the world, live miserable lives and have no hope of them becoming better. But anyone can see that their hopeless situation results from the actions of their fellow humans.

'Chaos', one of the few words drawn from mathematics to make an impact on popular speech, might give us a clue to the answer. A chaotic system is one whose future course of development is changed drastically by small inaccuracies in its present state. Predicting its trajectory in terms of any simple rule is utterly impossible. Its behaviour is best described as 'mad'. The world at the end of the millennium does indeed look like this. How is it possible for us to grasp its nature, let alone to determine or predict its future course?

The New World Order

In the summer of 1989, a much-hyped article called 'The End of History?' appeared in a US journal, *The National Interest*. Its author, Francis Fukuyama, announced that 'Liberalism' had defeated 'Communism' and that a new period of human development had begun. (When the same author's book *The End of History and the Last Man* appeared a year later, he had dispensed with the question mark in the title.) Armed with a few phrases from Hegel, Fukuyama tried to describe what was going to happen after the breaking of the Berlin Wall, when History had come to an end.

As the Stalinist regimes crumbled, the idea of a 'New World Order' became so fashionable that President George Bush made use of the phrase. He was particularly pleased with the idea that this new way of running the world demonstrated its value in the Gulf War. The ability of the United Nations to sanction what was effectively the US attack on Iraq, he assured the world, showed us the shape of future collaboration between the leading world powers, especially with the newly reconstructed Soviet Union.

It is a big idea, a new world order ... new ways of working with other nations, peaceful settlement of disputes, solidarity against aggression, reduced and controlled arsenals and just treatment of all nations.

Thus, in his usual elegant prose-style, the former head of the CIA explained the significance of the New World Order. Meanwhile, thousands of young Iraqi peasants were burned, crushed or blown apart by the latest products of civilisation. (According to *Newsweek*, 20 January 1992, 244 allied troops were killed in action, while Iraqi military casualties were estimated at around 100,000 dead, together with an unknown, but even larger, number of civilian deaths.)

The trouble with new phases of development is that there are only old categories in which to understand them, and these are, by definition, never adequate. The Gulf War was explained from many points of view, but always in unexamined terms from the past like 'imperialism', 'democracy', 'North–South divide', and so on. But what was happening could not be captured by these old phrases.

It is apt that the Gulf War was the occasion from which to date the onset of the new era, for it accurately characterised many aspects of the world as the century staggers to a close. For instance, the war was notable for the way that the television report was employed as a means of confusion. It is interesting that Saddam Hussein and George Bush regularly watched the same CNN bulletins throughout the conflict. Military spokesmen appeared in every living-room, in every country, delivering profound dollops of misinformation, and pointing with pride to those technological wonders which are such an important aspect of the New World Order. For example, they were particularly pleased with the ability which the new 'hardware' gave its users to kill large numbers of people without getting near enough to see them.

When Bush made his speech, he had in mind the willingness of the Soviet Union under Mikhail Gorbachev to collaborate in the US policing of the world, especially in the Middle East and in Southern Africa. And it is certainly true that, without this particular political situation, the US and allies could not have launched their 'Desert Storm'. But within a few months, not only Gorbachev and his government, but the Soviet Union itself, had vanished for ever.

As some features of the New World Order revealed themselves more clearly, people began to wonder whether its title was not somewhat misleading. It was certainly a *world* phenomenon, and it had many features which were *new*. But was it a form of *order*?

By January 1993, even UK Foreign Minister Douglas Hurd was talking of 'the continuing slide into disorder'. Using words like 'chaos and anarchy', he listed 25 conflicts raging at that time, referring in particular to Somalia, Yugoslavia, the Transcaucasus, Angola and Cambodia. Effectively contradicting the outgoing US President, Hurd declared that talk of a New World Order was 'utopian folly', and the phrase soon vanished from the editorial columns.

To qualify as an order, an entity needs some unifying principle. According to the experts on such matters, the Old World Order was founded on the antagonism of the two nuclear super-powers. This way of life, governed precariously by balancing the twin threats of atomic incineration (Mutually Assured Destruction, or MAD, as it was appropriately known), had now come to an end: only one of the two former super-powers was left.

Bush's idea of the New World Order was based on the expectation that the US was going to resume its singlehanded role as global sheriff. But many experts in international relations had already begun to discuss the decline of the US following its Vietnam defeat twenty years before. They began to speculate about a 'tri-polar' world set-up, in which Germany, dominating Europe, and Japan, in charge of Asia-Pacific, would vie with the Americans for world leadership.

Bush believed that his actions in the Middle East had shown the world how US hegemony could be restored. 'We've finally kicked the Vietnam syndrome', was the charming way he put it. However, the Gulf War gave us an illustration of this aspect, too, when the US and Japan came to blows over Japanese reluctance to hand over a sufficient amount of cash to pay for Bush's war. Only the US had the military power to fight such a war. However, as the largest debtor in the world, it could do so only with the financial backing of the world's largest creditor.

Another feature of the New World Order is the appearance of right-wing political movements, usually expressing violent racist and nationalist views, which has taken the world by surprise during the past few years. From the disintegrated Yugoslavia to the Indian subcontinent, from Rostock to Armenia, their brutalities have amazed the world, including many of the participants.

However close the parallels might seem, these eruptions cannot be comprehended in terms of past phenomena, for example, by analogy with pre-war fascism. In these movements of despair, movements without a future, both the cynicism of their leaders and the confusion of their followers have a uniquely contemporary character.

The disintegration of what was once Yugoslavia has combined all of these features in a terrifying way. National, religious and ethnic divisions whose origins are buried long in the past have erupted in brutal and mindless forms of struggle. They are fought out with the most up-to-date weaponry. The Great Powers' feeble attempts at intervention mask the efforts of each power to use the situation to its own advantage, often without any clear idea what that might be.

This 'New World Order' is an international regime characterised by confusion at every level. It is a world which evades comprehension, prediction or control.

Where are We Going?

So here we are in the last decade of what is generally counted as the second millennium. Human beings, equipped with the means to control the natural world, are bereft of the power to control their own lives. At the same time, they are in the grip of forms of thinking which make the resulting inhuman ways of living appear perfectly 'natural'. Since they lead increasingly fragmented lives, how can they possibly grasp the true nature of the situation as a whole?

More and more, thought is dominated by the certainty that there *is* no way out. The failure of all previous attempts to comprehend the whole picture is taken as proof that there is no such picture. It is not just that we do not know the truth: celebrated thinkers and artists declare with great authority that *there is no truth*. There are only what they call 'incommensurable' bits and pieces of 'discourse', some of which tell slightly smaller lies than others. That is why, at the very time when we need to speak as plainly as we can to each other and to ourselves, leading thinkers are determined to wrap their pronouncements in the most obscure language they can devise.

What is the nature of *homo sapiens*? How must we live to accord with that nature? Why do we not live like that already? Can we collectively alter our way of life, and, if so, how? What kind of knowledge is required to make this possible? This book is about a thinker whose ideas on questions like these have been ignored. He strove all his life to discover how humans could live in a way 'worthy of their human nature'. Nobody took any notice. His name was Karl Marx.

To some, this will sound very odd. The works of Marx have been printed in vast quantities and libraries are filled with commentaries on them. Doesn't 'everybody' know what Marxism was about? Yes, but as so often happens, 'everybody' is quite wrong.

In the name of 'Marxism', the Stalinist regimes forced their school children to study a body of doctrine shaped like a state religion. Ideas which were developed as part of the struggle for the liberation of mankind from exploitation and oppression were debased and used by cynical bureaucrats to find their way to promotion in an oppressive and inhuman state machine, and to hide their privileges. Presented as a complete, integral, 'scientific' body of knowledge, this theoretical monstrosity so sullied the ideas and even the vocabulary of Marx's work, that we are obliged to tunnel our way through a mass of this stuff to find out what Marx was actually trying to do.

I believe that this work is vital. I am not talking about formulating a new political programme, or finding a recipe to cure our economic ills. The problems which confront us go far too deep for that kind of measure. Nor am I interested in some academic efforts to clear up the historical record. The reason it is necessary to rediscover what Marx was really trying to do is that he did get to the heart of those very questions which confront all of us in the way we live today.

In this book, I try to show that all of Marx's major works – not just the work of 'the Young Marx', as some have thought – contain an investigation of questions such as: What is it to be human? In what ways are we estranged from our humanity? How can we live humanly? What must we do to make this possible? How must we think about the world to find the answers to these problems?

Of course, such questions have little in common with the 'Marxist' understanding of Marx, but then, as he said, he himself was no 'Marxist'.

2 How the 'Marxists' Buried Marx

What's certain is that I'm no Marxist.
Ce qu'il y a de certain, c'est que moi, je ne suis pas de Marxiste.

Karl Marx[1]

Marx and 'Marxism'

Many people these days will tell you 'Marxism is dead', usually with the collapse of the USSR in mind. There are still several varieties of 'Marxist' who deny it, of course. However, neither side shows much inclination to talk about the actual ideas whose death or survival are being disputed.

I believe that every current of thought since October 1917, however remote from that event it might appear, has reflected the problems raised by the Russian Revolution. For millions of working people, October shone a ray of hope on their lives, while for the ruling classes of the world it represented a mortal threat. However you looked at the problems of world society, whether from a factory bench or from a university philosophy department, whether you sought a radical change or were utterly hostile to socialism, the Soviet experiment was seen as *the* alternative to the existing social order.

When this attempt to establish a new way of life gave way to the bureaucratic monstrosity now universally associated with the name of Stalin, all forms of thought reflected the failure. Today, when little remains of this experiment, its outcome marks the way people think even more strongly. For many, the issue of socialism is now closed: you can't beat the system.

As I have already explained, I don't agree with them at all. On the contrary, while this may be a dreadful time to try to patch up bits and pieces of Marxism, it is precisely now, at last, that it is possible to look afresh at Marx's work and at the entire socialist project. The virtual disappearance of Stalinism has brought the freedom to question dogma long taken on trust, to ask ourselves what Marx was really trying to do and

even to read what he actually *wrote*. Re-examining texts that you
thought you knew all about often leads to quite surprising conclusions.

In a way, Marx's ideas have shared the fate of many other historical
figures. The following 'general heuristic principle' might not be too wide
of the mark: Let 'X' be any great thinker; then 'X'-ism, or 'X'-ianity,
or 'X'-ianism, will be in direct opposition to the ideas of 'X'. The case
of Jesus of Nazareth is too well known to require comment. A less
familiar example might be Isaac Newton. Books still appear telling the
innocent student about 'Newton's mechanical outlook'. Their authors
are incapable of acknowledging the historical research which has made
this picture quite untenable. It is now inescapable that the author of
Principia, founder of modern physics, was a continuator of the tradition
of alchemy, Cabalism, Hermetic magic and Arian theology, violently
opposed to the 'mechanical philosophy'.[2]

What frequently happens is this: the ideas of an original thinker are
first denounced as sheer madness. Then, after a decent interval, these
ideas are processed into a few sound-bites and assimilated into the
existing mind-set of the time, while their author is subjected to the most
absurd adulation. Finally, the unfortunate man or woman becomes a
household name, and 'everybody knows' what they 'really meant'.

After that, as you pick up one of their books and just look at the title-
page, you already 'know' what it is all about. Anything which contradicts
your original notion of the author's ideas can then be dismissed as an
aberration. They are now effectively silenced for the rest of time.
Safely dead, they can't stop their work being falsified in this way. It is
extremely difficult to get through to their ideas and to listen to what
they actually had to say.

In the case of Karl Marx, the obstacles preventing us from appreci-
ating his thought are reinforced with several extra protective layers.
'Marxism' is not just a doctrine, but a tradition, not just a set of theoretical notions, but the life activity of large numbers of people. These
men and women have invested their entire lives in fighting for what
they thought were the theories of Marx, convinced they were struggling
for the emancipation of humanity from exploitation and oppression.
Their theory was an attempt to give a coherent account of what was
happening in the world, including their own activity. It is a very
painful business for them to cut a path through the misconceptions on
which they had based their efforts. Not surprisingly, many find it much
easier to ditch the whole thing.

When I accuse 'Marxists' of burying Marx, I don't mean to condemn
attempts to develop older ideas to take account of new situations and

events – of course, that is legitimate. I am talking about the process whereby Marx's essential insights were obscured and denied.

Each generation of 'Marxists' inherited a set of ideas and defended it against its critics. As these opponents were, in general, utterly ignorant of what they purported to refute, their attacks only helped to shore up the prejudices of the 'Marxists'. Particular prominent figures in the movement became accepted as 'authorities', quotations from whose works would decide the issue in the event of dispute.

When Marxism became the doctrine claimed by large organisations, a canon of 'orthodoxy' was established. Anybody appearing to contradict standard texts or interpretations was perceived as an enemy. As happened to Jesus of Nazareth, too, the ideas of 'orthodox Marxism' became bound up with a massive state structure. Soon, orthodoxy was protected by state power, with all its sanctions of isolation, exile, violence and death.

That is why, if we want to find out what Marx's ideas have to say about the contemporary world, we can't do it just by reading his books. We have to retrace the path by which the tradition came into being, to find out how and where Marx was buried. I am certainly not the only one today trying to re-examine this history. Some people want to 'reconstruct Marxism'. Others are also trying to discover and correct the distortions which are now so evident. Each of these people must base their work on his or her own experience. Some of this work is useful,[3] but I think little of it digs very deep.

In this chapter, I try to retrace my own steps and attempt to find my way back to Marx's actual ideas. Let me repeat, I am not looking for the 'genuine', 'pure', 'perfect', 'original' Marx, who will provide us with the 'correct' answers – such a person never existed. I want to establish what were Marx's real ideas, in order to see what they have to say about our present predicament.

Even in their lifetimes, Marx (1818–1883) and Engels (1820–1895) were dismayed to see their fundamental notions buried under the myth of infallibility. Marx would have been utterly hostile to the statement of Plekhanov (1856–1918) that 'Marxism is an integral world outlook'.[4] In fact, only a fraction of Marx's original plan for his work was ever completed. By the time of his death, bourgeois society was already entering a new stage. A large and important part of his writings remained as unedited and undeciphered manuscripts, unknown even to Engels.

The early work of Marx began to become widely available from the turn of the century. As late as the 1960s and 1970s, important works were still appearing. The difficulty of making this material fit in with the 'orthodox' picture was dealt with by attributing it to someone called 'the Young Marx'.

If you imagine this was a young chap in short trousers and schoolboy cap, consider that in 1844, when he wrote the *Paris Manuscripts*, Marx was a 26-year-old married man with a child, who had already lost one job as the editor of a major journal. In any case, the long manuscript known as *Grundrisse*, written when the author was 40 years old, contradicts the 'orthodox' view as sharply as anything he was writing fifteen years earlier. Marx's work in the last decade of his life is also most troublesome for the 'orthodox' story.

Of course, in nearly half a century of Marx's political struggle and scientific work, there are inconsistencies, digressions and mistakes. But his life had one central aim: to fight for the emancipation of humanity. He strove to find a path to a world without exploitation or oppression, in which men and women developed their human potential as free individuals in a free society, without the distortion of money or state power.

He believed that the liberation of humanity would centre on the movement of the working class to liberate itself. He was devoted to democratic forms and had no time for centralised, disciplined political organisations, operating behind the backs of the mass of working people. He was utterly opposed to the idea of self-appointed leaders, however well intentioned, setting up a strong state. And yet this struggle for human freedom became identified with its direct opposite. How could that happen?

I am not trying to write a history of the socialist movement. By looking back at some episodes in the development of the 'Marxist' myth, I want to focus on its philosophical foundations. Instead of moving chronologically through the decades, I am going to take four slices of history, starting with the most recent:

- the formation of the Stalinised version, known falsely as 'Marxism-Leninism';
- the outlook of the Communist International;
- the 'orthodoxy' of the Second International before 1914, and its relation to the work of Engels;
- Karl Marx's attitude to 'Marxism'.

I hope, by stripping away the layers of distortion and misunderstanding deposited by these episodes, to clear the way to re-examine Marx's actual notions. Three themes keep appearing in the story: the way history moves, the nature of the state and the role of a revolutionary party.

The Philosophy of Thuggery

Since this book is about the importance of Marx's insights for the tasks of human liberation, it is appropriate to begin with one of the most widely circulated philosophical statements of the twentieth century. It starts like this:

> Dialectical materialism is the outlook of the Marxist-Leninist party. It is called dialectical materialism because its approach to the phenomena of nature, its method of apprehending them is *dialectical*, while its interpretation of the phenomena of nature, its conception of these phenomena, its theory, is *materialistic*.
>
> Historical materialism is the extension of the principles of dialectical materialism to the study of social life, an application of the principles of dialectical materialism to the phenomena of the life of society, to the study of society and of its history.[5]

This stuff appeared in 1939. In my view, its method, standpoint, dogmatic style and conclusions are all utterly opposed to everything that Marx stood for. Large numbers of people, some of them very clever, hailed it as a work of genius. The most important thing to know about it is that its author was responsible for the murder and torture of millions of people, many of whom considered themselves to be Marxists.

Although *Dialectical and Historical Materialism*, by J.V. Stalin (1879–1953), goes on to quote extensively from the works of Engels and Lenin, and even some of Marx, a vast, blood-filled gulf separates it from these writers. It was an obscene caricature, which raised an enormous barrier to comprehending Marx's work, not just for the devotees of Stalinism, but for everybody else too.

Stalin's pseudo-philosophical document was extracted from the infamous *History of the CPSU (Bolsheviks): Short Course*, prepared by a Commission of the Central Committee. For eighteen years, this volume of lies and slanders formed the basis of all educational work in the USSR, and of all 'theory' in the world communist movement. In 1956, at the CPSU (Communist Party of the Societ Union) Twentieth Congress, it was announced that 'historical inaccuracies' had been discovered in it, and it was simply decided to withdraw it from circulation.

This was not so easy, however. These pages embodied the basic notions on which the leaders of Communist Parties and several then-powerful states tried to find justification for their actions. That is why many devout 'Marxist-Leninists' were incapable of carrying out the decision, denying the authority of Moscow for the first time in their lives.

In 1939, the insertion of this 'philosophical' section was essential to Stalin's purpose in issuing the *Short Course*. (He made some other 'suggestions' for additional material, but they were mainly to increase the lying abuse of his enemies and to glorify the image of himself still further.) By that time, the last of the Old Bolsheviks, those who had led the 1917 Revolution, had been humiliated in the Moscow Show Trials, and had been forced to 'confess' to the most fantastic crimes. They were shot or sent to perish in the Gulags. The last vestiges of independent thought had been eliminated.

The ruling group around Stalin felt it necessary to take command of every aspect of life and knowledge. The bureaucracy's political organisation went under the name of 'Communist Party', or 'Party of the proletariat'. The original leaders of the organisation of that name had been effectively wiped out by the secret-police thugs of the 'philosopher' Stalin.

The name of Marx was now obscenely linked with the 'theory' of this Party. In that terrible time, the very terms 'socialism' and 'communism' came to be identified with this monstrosity. But even for those who could see what a falsification this was, the ideas of Marx became inextricably fouled up in the network of bureaucratic assumptions, including terms like 'workers' state', 'revolutionary party', and 'orthodox theory'. The name of Marx, who stood for the liberation of mankind from exploitation and the disappearance of state oppression, became entangled with the defence of the privileges of a bureaucratic caste and the power of a brutal state apparatus.

'Dialectical materialism' – also known as 'Diamat', the original of Orwell's 'Newspeak' – expressed the ideological needs of this bureaucracy. In *Dialectical and Historical Materialism*, Stalin attached these words to a set of pseudo-philosophical notions, which became for many people a form of religious belief. It was forced down the throats of Soviet school children as the state religion, and it was the obligatory creed of members of Stalinist parties the world over.

The doctrine here called 'materialism' opposes a mechanically interpreted nature – 'objectivity' – to all subjective thought, will and feeling, which are declared to be 'secondary', 'determined' by this 'material world'. In this bureaucratic script, human beings were cast as puppets controlled by an impersonal historical process.

Not all of them, though. Into this nightmare was inserted a body called the 'revolutionary party', whose leaders were somehow exempt from the influence of material forces. A set of rules called 'dialectics' explained how these leaders could change their decisions at will. The bureaucrats were the proprietors of History.

During the previous decade, even while the Stalinisation of the Comintern was taking place, a certain kind of philosophical discussion had still been possible and, in the late 1920s, a war began between two groups of Soviet philosophers. On the one side stood those who leant heavily on some of Lenin's notes, which their leader Deborin had discovered after Lenin's death. This group emphasised the importance of Hegel (1770–1831) and 'dialectics'. Against them, the 'mechanists' were devoted to 'materialism'. They also cited Lenin: his 1908 book *Materialism and Empirio-Criticism*. Each side claimed that its 'line' was more 'correct', that is, more attuned to the current requirements of the Stalin leadership.

In January 1931 this dispute was finally settled. Stalin himself intervened at a meeting of the CPSU Central Committee. A certain M.B. Mitin became the authority on all things philosophical. As he explained so well: 'The further advancement of Marxist-Leninist theory in every department, including that of the philosophy of Marxism, is associated with the name of Comrade Stalin.'[6]

The mechanists were denounced as followers of the recently demoted Bukharin, while the Deborinites were now discovered to be 'Menshevising idealists'. Within a few years, many of each of these groups were dead, and so were some of those who had displaced them. While this meeting was taking place, millions of Soviet peasants were being starved to death and entire nations were being transported thousands of miles from their homes in cattle-trucks.

Let us bring ourselves to look briefly at the way the Stalinist catechism of 1939 hitched up a highly mechanised materialism with something called 'dialectics'. On the one hand, 'Nature, being, the material world, is primary, and mind, thought, is secondary.'[7] What does this word 'primary' mean? Does it mean 'first in time' or 'first in importance'? Or does it mean that matter 'causes' changes in 'mind'? Nobody can tell, and precisely this ambiguity conferred mysterious power.

On the other hand, 'dialectical laws of development' were somehow extracted from the system of G.W.F. Hegel – who was, however, an 'idealist', which meant a mirror-image of the kind of 'materialist' referred to just now. This was a reference to Engels's 'three laws of dialectics'. (But great problems were caused for the faithful when it was found that, after 'the passage of quantity into quality' and 'the struggle of opposites', Stalin had forgotten the third of Engels's 'laws', the 'law of the negation of negation'.)

This utterly dehumanised way of thinking was now ready to be 'applied' to human history:

> The material life of society, its being, is also primary, and its spiritual reality secondary, derivative. ... The material life of society is an objective reality existing independently of the will of men, while the spiritual life of society is a reflection of this objective reality, a reflection of being.
>
> Hence social life, the history of society, ceases to be an agglomeration of 'accidents' and becomes the history of the development of society according to regular laws, and the study of history becomes a science. ... Hence the practical activity of the party of the proletariat must ... be based ... on the laws of development of society ... and the data of science regarding the laws of development of society are authentic data having the validity of objective truths.[8]

There is a 'force' which 'determines' the 'physiognomy' of society: 'This force, historical materialism holds, is the method of procuring the means of life necessary for human existence, the mode of production of material values – food, clothing, footware, houses, fuel, instruments of production, etc.'[9]

On this theoretical foundation – the only 'correct' one, of course – it could be asserted that: 'five main types of relations of production are known to history: primitive communal, slave, feudal, capitalist and socialist'.[10] The last of these five has already arrived:

> The basis of the relations of production under the Socialist system, which so far has been established only in the USSR, is the social ownership of the means of production. Here there are no longer exploiters and exploited. The goods produced are distributed according to labour performed, on the principle: 'He who does not work, neither shall he eat'. Here the mutual relations of people in the process of production are marked by comradely cooperation and the Socialist mutual assistance of workers who are free from exploitation.[11]

Under the name 'Marxism-Leninism', and with the 'scientific' authority of the secret police and its torture chambers, the bureaucracy decided what was 'correct'. They, the proprietors of 'the dialectic', decided what the 'laws of history' held in store for 'workers who are free from exploitation'. Living at a level far removed from the desperate poverty of the mass of Soviet workers and peasants, protected by a massive security apparatus, the bureaucrats administered the 'distribution according to labour performed'. As Trotsky explained, in *The Revolution Betrayed*, those with the power to decide on this distribution began by grabbing their own giant share.

Is it really necessary to be reminded of this nightmare 'world-outlook'? Unfortunately, it is, in order to re-examine the ideas of Marx. For it became impossible to view Marx's work unless it was first refracted through the distorting lens of this tradition. For example, it is depressing to note that a thinker of the stature of Jurgens Habermas can describe Stalin's essay as 'a handbook of historical materialism'.[12]

Even those who fought against the murder-machine which was ideologically lubricated by this stuff could not escape being affected by it. Trotsky (1879–1940) and his supporters struggled to maintain the outlook which inspired and guided the Russian Revolution and the formation of the Communist International. With whatever voice they had, they denounced the lies and corruption of Stalinism – especially the lie that Stalin's Russia was 'socialism'. But they never had the theoretical resources to penetrate to its philosophical core. The best they could do was to show that Stalinist policies and distortions were contrary to the decisions of Lenin's party and the teachings of 'Marxism'.

Throughout the 1930s, Trotsky, while never claiming any special philosophical knowledge, continually but vainly implored his followers to undertake the study of such matters. When, under the terrible conditions of exile, he tried to continue with his planned biography of Lenin, he found it necessary to study Hegel's *Science of Logic*. He managed to get through about 30 pages before being forced to turn to other questions.[13]

At best, the Trotskyists could strive to defend an existing body of theory. Trotsky's great article *Stalinism and Bolshevism*, which he wrote in 1937, begins like this:

> Reactionary epochs like ours not only disintegrate and weaken the working class and isolate its vanguard but also lower the general ideological level of the movement and throw it back to stages long since passed through. In these conditions the task of the vanguard is above all not to let itself be carried along by the backward flow: it must swim against the current. If an unfavourable relation of forces prevents it from holding the positions it has won, it must at least retain its ideo-

logical positions, because in them is expressed the dearly-paid experience of the past. Fools will consider this policy 'sectarian'. In fact it is the only means of preparing for a new tremendous surge forward with the coming historical tide.[14]

But defence of an established set of ideas, however heroic, proved to be quite inadequate.

Trotsky refused to accept the often-parrotted notion that Stalinism was the inevitable continuation of Lenin's work. This idea, now more fashionable than ever, actually explains nothing. The false ideas of one person cannot be explained simply by the false ideas of another. However, what is true is that, when Stalin erected his massive historical road-block to communism, he exploited to the full every weakness contained in the outlook of Lenin's party. Unless we investigate these defects as thoroughly as we can, it will prove impossible to find our way through.

Philosophy and the Russian Revolution

In 1917, the Soviets took over the government of what had been the Tsarist Empire, under the leadership of the organisation which now renamed itself the Communist Party. For the first time, working men and women took the struggle for control over their own lives to the level of capturing the state power. Almost without precedent, this movement of the small and inexperienced Russian working class pointed to a way out of the hell of the World War.

The success of this attempt was predicated on the rapid spread of the revolution to Germany and other industrialised countries. With the help of the more advanced working-class movements, the Soviets could transform their economically and culturally backward peasant country, devastated by the imperialist war. Its aim of establishing socialism would be realised on a European and world scale.

With the disappointment of these hopes, huge problems arose. The determination of the Bolshevik leaders to confront and not to evade them remains one of the great stories of the twentieth century. But, however great my admiration for their struggles, I am obliged to look with great care at their effect on the way we see ourselves today.

When it was a matter of the Revolution holding on by all possible means for a few weeks or months, the devotion and courage of the Soviet workers and their allies inside and outside the former Tsarist Empire could be sustained. But when these months stretched into years and even decades, the question appeared in quite a different shape.

In 1919, the Communist International, 'World Party of Socialist Revolution', came into being, winning the allegiance of the best sections of the working class throughout the world. The Communists insisted that ruthless and violent struggle was required to destroy the political power of capital. They counterposed this to the conception of peaceful, parliamentary transformation, to which the ruling class would quietly submit, the view attributed to their enemies, the Social Democratic leaders.

But by that time, the idea of the 'dictatorship of the proletariat' had been changed into something quite new. To Marx this phrase meant that the functions of the state would be taken into the hands of the whole of the working class, preparatory to its dissolution in a free community. When this was seen to be out of the question in backward Russia, the Communists invented something called a 'workers' state' – a term not used by Marx, nor by any of his followers before 1918 – to describe the bureaucratic machine whose tentacles were already taking hold of the heart of the Revolution. (As far as I can tell, the phrase first appeared when communists begin to discuss the 'bureaucratic deformations' of the Soviet state. There is more about this in Chapter 3.)

Without such an apparatus, the survival of the Revolution would have been impossible. How else could you win a civil war against enemies who had massive support from the most powerful imperialist states? Yes, but with this apparatus, what was it that survived?

I shall argue that behind the thinking of the Bolsheviks stood notions of the state and of the Party which blocked the path to any understanding of what was happening. This can be seen, for example, in these extracts from a book which was widely read in the 'heroic' days of the Revolution and the Civil War:

> In the hands of the Party is concentrated the general control. ... It has the final word in all fundamental questions. ... The last word rests with the Central Committee. ... We have more than once been accused of having substituted for the dictatorship of the soviets the dictatorship of our party. Yet it can be said with complete justice that the dictatorship of the soviets became possible only by means of the dictatorship of the party.[15]

> We oppose capitalist slavery by socially-regulated labour. ... Wages ... must be brought into the closest possible touch with the productivity of individual labour. Under capitalism, the system of

piece-work and of grading, the application of the Taylor system, etc.,
have as their object to increase the exploitation of the workers by the
squeezing out of surplus value. Under socialist production, piece-work,
bonuses, etc., have as their problem to increase the volume of social
product, and consequently to raise the general well-being. Those
workers who do more for the general interest receive the right to a
greater quantity of the social product than the lazy, the careless and
the disorganisers.[16]

Just as a lamp before going out shoots up a brilliant flame, so the state
before disappearing assumes the form of the dictatorship of the proletariat, the most ruthless form of state, which embraces the life of the
citizens authoritatively in every direction.[17]

Leon Trotsky wrote these lines early in 1920, in the armoured train
from which he directed the victories of the Red Army over the armies
sent by the imperialists. The pamphlet *Terrorism and Communism*, from
which I have extracted them – somewhat unfairly, because their author
had many other things to say in it – was representative of Comintern
thinking at the time. Each delegate to the Second Congress of the International was given a copy, together with Lenin's *Left-Wing Communism*.
(It certainly does not represent Trotsky's attitude after 1923. However,
I am sorry to say that, when Trotsky re-issued it in English in 1935 and
in French in 1936, he gave his readers no ideological health warning.)

By 1920, the international isolation of the Revolution was already
beginning to have its dire effect on the theory of the communist
movement. Lenin and Trotsky, as well as other leaders of the International, struggled to find a theoretical framework within which to tackle
the terrible economic and social issues facing the Soviet state. But, as I
shall show, 'Marxism' as they understood it already formed a barrier,
walling them off from Marx himself.

In his last writings, the dying Lenin battled with the growing forces
of the Soviet state bureaucracy, now gaining ground within the
Communist Party itself and in the International. He frequently posed
the problem of how to 'draw the masses into the administration of the
State'. But who were those who sought to do the 'drawing'? What had
happened to the idea of the self-emancipation of the working class, and
of the 'dying-out of the state', which Lenin himself had rediscovered
in 1917? Lenin did not try to hide from these excruciating questions,
raised by the harsh reality of the Civil War. He referred more than once
to the 'declassing' of the tiny Russian working class in the course of the

Civil War and its aftermath, and pointed out the perils this implied for
the future of the Party.

By 1919, the soviets, the organs of mass democratic action which
sprang up in 1917, had vanished in all but name. Many thousands of
those workers who had been to the fore in 1917 had perished in the
course of the Civil War. The 'dictatorship of the proletariat' had been
transformed into a kind of spiritual force directed by the Party and its
leadership, independently of the will or knowledge of the human
beings actually struggling to live in those terrible days. Stalin later
completed the work of destroying that generation and replaced the Party
with a bureaucratic machine.

Lenin Canonised

However unpopular the idea may be in some circles today, I still
believe that V.I. Lenin was the greatest individual figure of our century.
In his own life and thought, he concentrated the world-wide striving
of millions for emancipation. So I approach the task of re-examining
his theoretical work with trepidation. Everything he wrote is of great
importance. But if it is accepted as biblical authority – and he would
have denounced any attempt to treat it as such – it will be impossible
to find a way through the confusion surrounding Marx's ideas.

Stalin's canonisation of Lenin was an essential part of the destruction
of Marx's method – that method Marx had declared 'lets nothing
impose upon it and is in its essence critical and revolutionary'.[18] It is
ironical to read in this context Lenin's words of 1917:

> What is now happening to Marx's theory has, in the course of
> history, happened repeatedly to the theories of revolutionary thinkers
> and leaders of oppressed classes fighting for emancipation. During the
> lifetime of great revolutionaries, the oppressing classes constantly
> hounded them, received their theories with the most savage malice,
> the most furious hatred and the most unscrupulous campaigns of lies
> and slander. After their death, attempts are made to convert them into
> harmless icons.[19]

Once the embalmed body of Lenin had been stuck in the mausoleum,
his writings, editorially embalmed, were pressed into the service of the
ruling caste. Contrary to every tradition of Bolshevism and of Marx's ideas,
it soon became impossible to question any approved text of Lenin.

In the worst traditions of religious bigotry, some of Lenin's writings
had to be suppressed, in particular his 1922 *Letter to the Congress*, known
as 'Lenin's Testament', with its postscript calling for Stalin's removal.

But even those of his works which were printed by the million had their
revolutionary spirit crushed under the weight of pious commentary and
lying footnotes.

Bukharin, the Mechanical Revolutionary

Until 1924, Nicolai Bukharin (1888–1938) was the leader of the left-
wing of Lenin's party, often very critical of its policies. One of the most
popular of Party leaders, he stood for the immediate implementation
of the measures that Lenin had discussed theoretically in his pamphlet
The State and Revolution, written in the heady days of 1917. He was also
one of the very few leading Bolsheviks who took an interest in philosophical matters.

In 1919, assisted by the young economist E.A. Preobrazhensky
(1886–1937), he wrote a commentary on the newly agreed Programme
of the Party. Issued under the title *The ABC of Communism*, it was a best-
seller among the communists of many countries. Its Utopian conceptions
were presented with all of Bukharin's undoubted charm and clarity. But
they make spine-chilling reading in the light of the history of the past
seventy years.

This is what Bukharin thinks Marx's theory is all about:

> Marx … examined the evil, unjust, barbaric social order which still
> prevails throughout the world, and studied its structure. Precisely after
> the manner in which we might study a machine or, let us say, a clock,
> did Marx study the structure of capitalist society, in which landlords
> and factory-owners rule, while workers and peasants are oppressed.
> Let us suppose that we have noticed that two of the wheels of our
> clock are badly fitted, and that at each revolution they interfere
> more and more with one another's movements. Then we can foresee
> that the clock will break down and stop. … Marx recognised very
> clearly that capitalism is digging its own grave, that the machine will
> break down, and that the cause of the break-down will be the
> inevitable uprising of the workers, who will refashion the whole world
> to suit themselves.[20]

This way of looking at the world, Bukharin explains, is 'scientific'.
Communism, he is quite sure, is a system in which the parts of the
mechanism are much better 'mutually adapted'. It will be a society which
is 'organised throughout'.

Bukharin recommends the dictatorship of the proletariat as the only
way to make the transition to the classless society, and explains that '"dictatorship" signifies strict method of government and a resolute crushing

of enemies'.[21] On the other hand, he quotes the new Constitution to confirm that this dictatorship is only a transitory form.[22]

In 1920, Bukharin completed his theoretical justification of these ideas in *Historical Materialism*, which remained in print for a decade. He explains the difference between 'proletarian science' and 'bourgeois science' by analogy: we can either view the world through red eyeglasses or through white ones. His 'system' of 'Marxian sociology' runs on purely mechanical lines, which is how he understands 'science'.[23]

Cause and effect are his chief categories. The clash of opposing forces, the resultant of many wills, results in equilibrium. Reality moves through a cycle in which the disturbance of each equilibrium gives rise to a new one. The meaning of historical materialism is for him 'social determinism', while society is a system of interactions between its 'elements'.

Towards the end of 1920, a dispute broke out in the Bolshevik Party on the role of the trade unions in the Soviet economy, which reveals some of the difficulties faced by the Bolsheviks in understanding their own state. Trotsky and Bukharin each proposed that the unions be absorbed into the economic planning machinery. The argument was simple: if the unions operate under a workers' state, against whom do they need to protect their members? But Lenin denounced this argument as 'abstraction':

> For one thing, ours is not actually a workers' state but a workers' and peasants' state. ... We now have a state under which it is the business of the massively organised proletariat to protect itself, while we, for our part, must use these workers' organisations to protect the workers from their state and to get them to protect our state.[24]

When Lenin was speaking, Bukharin interrupted this characterisation of the Soviet state as a 'workers' and peasants' state', and, in a later article in *Pravda*, Lenin answered him.

> I was wrong and Comrade Bukharin was right. What I should have said is: 'A workers' state is an abstraction. What we actually have is a workers' state with this peculiarity, firstly, that it is not the working class but the peasant population that predominates in the country, and secondly, that it is a workers' state with bureaucratic distortions.'[25]

These remarks have often been quoted, but I think they should be examined again. Of course, they display Lenin's amazing flexibility of thought and his refusal to evade the most awkward difficulties for his own viewpoint. But look at how he describes the relation between the Soviet state and the working class. The leaders of the Communist Party must regard the Soviet state as 'our' state. If 'we' can 'use' the workers' organisations to protect the workers from 'our' state, 'we' will get them, in return, to protect 'our' state. All of this is contained in Lenin's remarkable formulation: 'Our state is not a workers' state, as Trotsky abstractly employed the term, but a "workers' state with bureaucratic distortions".'[26]

What happened after this dispute? Trotsky became the leader of the struggle, begun by Lenin, against the bureaucratisation of the state and the Party. As the bureaucratic machine strangled the remnants of the October Revolution, and indeed incorporated the trade unions into the state, Trotsky carried on this fight until Stalin's assassin killed him. Bukharin became the leader of the Right, showing how his mechanistic conceptions were equally suited to this new role. After Lenin's death, he became Stalin's chief ally, helping him to defeat the Left opposition. Having used him, Stalin destroyed him, first politically and eventually physically.

A Philosophical 'Discussion'

In 1923, the Hungarian communist Georgi Lukacs (1885–1971), then a leader of the 'leftist' faction, published his book *History and Class Consciousness*. Aimed against 'the Marxism of the Second International' – that is, 'Marxism' as it had been understood before 1917 – it attacked the mechanical ideas of Bukharin. It was also directly opposed to the 'materialism' of the earlier Lenin – although it never says so. It stressed the origins of Marx's work, especially *Capital*, in the philosophy of G.W.F. Hegel, and it contained a famous attack on Engels's conception of a 'dialectics of nature'.[27] At the same time, a leading German communist, Karl Korsch (1889–1961), published his *Communism and Philosophy*, with a somewhat similar outlook.

A fierce dispute broke out, in which Lukacs and Korsch were attacked for 'idealism'. At the Fifth World Congress of the International in 1924, Zinoviev (1883–1936), then President of the International and allied with Stalin against Trotsky, spoke on 'The Struggle against the Ultra-lefts and Theoretical Revisionism'. He included a characteristic onslaught on the two authors and those intellectuals who supported them. In line with his 'Bolshevisation' campaign, then in full swing, he denounced them as 'professors', a species he counterposed to 'honest workers': 'If we get a few more of these professors spinning out their Marxist theories, we shall be lost. We cannot tolerate theoretical revisionism of this kind in our communist international.'[28] Bukharin, soon to replace Zinoviev as Stalin's ally, is reported to have declared in conversation with Korsch and other delegates: 'Comrades, we cannot put every piece of garbage up for discussion.'[29]

The ideas of Korsch and Lukacs, instead of being combated in open debate, were answered with bureaucratic crudity. It is doubtful whether Zinoviev ever bothered to look at the books he was denouncing. Their authors' responses were interesting. Lukacs made his recantation, the first of many. Soon afterwards he wrote his essay, *Lenin, a Study in the Unity of his Thought* (1924),which opened the way for a new 'orthodoxy' called 'Leninism' – really a code name for Stalinism. Korsch also continued for a time to defend the current Comintern line, attacking both 'Trotskyism' and 'Luxemburgism' on behalf of 'Leninism'. In 1926, however, he developed left-wing criticisms of Stalin's line and was soon thrown out of both the German Party and the International.

The new 'approach' to theory, very different from the vigorous inner disputes of the movement in Lenin's time, was already taking shape. In Stalin's capable hands, this was transformed into a regime where nobody could question any action of the leadership – until the current line had been switched.

In the 1930s, the Frankfurt School, including Marcuse, Adorno, Horkheimer and others, tried to develop some aspects of Lukacs's approach. With the rise of Nazism in Germany, they lost faith in the possibility of a socialist transformation. For them and their successors, Marxism became no more than an academic effort to maintain the traditions of the Enlightenment.

Trotsky and Lenin

In the nightmare conditions under which Trotsky had to fight from 1923 onwards, he was forced to make difficult tactical decisions. One of them was to try to minimise his earlier differences with Lenin, not only where he thought Lenin's view was later proved correct, but sometimes also when it was wrong. This was understandable in view of the monstrous campaign of slander against him – but it is inexcusable for anyone today.

A remark Trotsky made in 1933 is illuminating in this connection. It was in a conversation with the writer Fritz Sternberg, who had his own disagreements with Lenin. Sternberg reports:

One day, when we were discussing Russian problems, he said: 'Stalin and the Stalinists are always trying to brand me as an anti-Leninist. It's a dirty slander, of course. I had profound differences with Lenin,

before, during, and after the Revolution and in the vital Civil War
years agreement always predominated between us.' Pursuing this
theme, Trotsky declared that he had no wish to present his opponents
in Russia with a new weapon by adopting a stance against Lenin's
views on the workers' aristocracy. Once he had made it clear that,
if only for tactical reasons, he did not wish to attack Lenin's position
on this question, we abandoned the subject.[30]

Today there is no such choice. We must look closely, in particular, at
Lenin's conception of a revolutionary party, its relation to the class it
strives to lead and the nature of the form of state which emerged from
its victory. Above all, we must re-examine his conception of the status
of the theory of such a party, its origin and the criteria for its validity.

'Marxism' in the Second International

Kautsky and 'Revisionism'
In 1889, the attempts to rebuild an international workers' organisation
after the defeat of the Paris Commune finally bore fruit. This was six
years after the death of Karl Marx, and 17 years after the International
Workingmen's Association ('First International') had faded away.

By that time, the socialist movement included several mass organisations, of which the German Social Democratic Party (SPD) was the
most significant. Of course, the most prominent figure in the 'Second
International', as it became, was Frederick Engels. (I shall say more about
him later.) But, from his death in 1895 until 1914, the SPD leaders gave
the International its main direction.

That is how the outlook of Karl Kautsky (1854–1938), theoretical
leader of the SPD, came to shape what became known as 'orthodox
Marxism'. Kautsky placed great emphasis on the 'scientific' character
of this orthodoxy. He saw the movement to socialism as being guaranteed
by the operation of 'laws of history'. These resembled laws of nature,
in that they operated independently of human will and consciousness.
They applied universally and used human beings as their instruments.
Their study was a science called 'historical materialism', or 'the materialist conception of history'.

Kautsky had already reduced *Capital* to a set of 'economic doctrines',
completely unconnected with the idea of communism.[31] He believed
these doctrines showed how the economic expansion of capitalist
production brought about both the development of technology and the

growth and concentration of the proletariat. Armed with the scientific doctrines of 'Marxism', the 'Marxist Party' had the task of bringing the truth to the masses. The socialist intellectuals would teach scientific socialism to the workers.

For Kautsky, he and people like him had gained possession of this truth through the work of science, so it was not possible for lesser mortals to steer the same course. But he never doubted that the organised workers, under this leadership, would eventually form a force large enough and sufficiently organised to ensure the disappearance of capitalism.

This was Kautsky's 'Road to Power'. What he called the socialist revolution was to be a long, drawn-out affair, punctuated by 'political revolutions'. Socialism meant chiefly that industry would come under the centralised control of the state, a state he envisaged as a form of advanced parliamentarism.

The SPD grew stronger, withstanding the years of Bismark's anti-socialist laws and becoming an increasingly successful electoral force. Now, other trends became more vocal among its leaders. Edward Bernstein (1850–1932), while he was exiled in London, became enamoured of the Fabian ideas of gradualism. Together with some other protégés of Engels, he began to question the very basis of Kautsky's 'orthodoxy'.

In 1897, Bernstein announced that Kautsky's conception of socialist revolution – he called it Marx's – was now outmoded. Capitalism would be peacefully and gradually transformed into socialism. The theory of surplus value had been superseded. Dialectics was no more than mysticism, and materialism an old-fashioned prejudice. The movement towards socialism would get on better if it ditched Marx's 'Hegelianism' in favour of the 'return to Kant', so fashionable in academic circles at that time. To get socialist policies adopted in Germany, it would be necessary to form alliances with Liberal critics of the Empire.

Kautsky had the job of fighting off this attack on 'orthodoxy'. Fairly politely, and after some hesitation, he reaffirmed what he thought Marx had said about the development of capitalism leading to socialism. But Bernstein was only giving a theoretical voice to what many leading Social Democrat parliamentarians and trade union wheeler-dealers already silently believed. They cared nothing about theoretical niceties, as long as they could get on with the 'real' politics – and with their careers.

Rosa Luxemburg (1871–1919) spoke for a new and younger group of left-wingers. Her answer to Bernstein, *Social Reform or Revolution?*, went much deeper than Kautsky's. In it, she demonstrated brilliantly that 'revisionism' represented an opportunist adaptation to bourgeois society. But nowhere did she approach the philosophical basis of the problem. Indeed, in the vast output of books and articles which she contributed to the international movement she displayed little interest in such matters. The truth of 'Marxism' was taken for granted as a body of doctrine by her as much as by Kautsky. And, as firmly as Kautsky, she thought that *Capital* was about the 'economic structure of capitalism'.

In the Tsarist Empire, a working class was developing, and with it an illegal but growing workers' movement. Georgi Plekhanov, in exile in Switzerland, had gathered around him a group of intellectuals who strove to build a socialist organisation, which claimed to be based on Marxism. Lenin, despite some occasional organisational differences, founded his theoretical ideas on those of Plekhanov and Kautsky.

Plekhanov himself became a leading defender of 'orthodoxy' in the International, impatiently pressing Kautsky to step up his attacks on the philosophical foundations of Bernstein's 'revisionism'. Kautsky could not get anywhere near the core of Bernstein's attack. In a letter to Plekhanov in 1898 the theoretical leader of the International declared:

> I have never been strong on philosophy. Although I stand entirely on the point of view of dialectical materialism, still I think that the economic and historical viewpoint of Marx and Engels is in the last resort compatible with neo-Kantianism.[32]

For Plekhanov, Marx's materialism was crucial. We shall see later the huge distance which separated Plekhanov's 'orthodox' views from what Marx actually thought.

Philosophy and Bolshevism

Right from the start of the dispute in the International, Lenin and his comrades were firm supporters of Kautsky. It is true that the illegal organisations of Russian revolutionaries had little in common with the 'official' bodies of social democracy in the more advanced countries. But in their theoretical work, they never strayed far from the 'orthodox' leadership.

Among the Russian 'Marxists' trying to organise the illegal Russian Social Democratic Labour Party (RSDLP), Lenin was very keen on fighting the 'Economist' tendency which sought to elevate 'spontaneous' trade-union ('economic') struggles above all theory. Lenin connected this issue with the effort to replace the 'circle' spirit which dominated the illegal Marxist movement with an organisation of 'professional revolutionaries', which would be capable of mobilising the young Russian working class to lead the overthrow of Tsarism.

However, in the course of this fight, Lenin tied himself to the most extreme theoretical position he could find, as he often did, and this appeared most strongly in his book *What is to be Done?*, issued in 1902. Taking the ideas of his leader Kautsky only a bit further, he brought out their implications. He contended that Marxist theory cannot arise 'spontaneously' in the working class, but must be brought into the labour movement by bourgeois intellectuals, 'from without'.

> The history of all countries shows that the working class, exclusively by its own effort, is able to develop only trade-union consciousness, ie the conviction that it is necessary to combine in unions, fight the employers, and strive to compel the government to pass necessary labour legislation, etc. The theory of socialism, however, grew out of the philosophic, historical, and economic theories elaborated by educated representatives of the propertied classes, by intellectuals. By their social status, the founders of modern socialism, Marx and Engels, belonged to the bourgeois intelligentsia.
>
> The task of Social Democracy is *to combat spontaneity*, to *divert* the working-class movement from this spontaneous, trade-unionist striving to come under the wing of the bourgeoisie, and to bring it under the wing of revolutionary Social-Democracy.[33]

Nothing like this is to be found in the writings of Marx or Engels. All their lives, they fought against those who built sects which aimed to show the world what it should be like. Instead, they declared that communism was 'the movement of the immense majority, in the interests of the immense majority'.[34] Only the working class could achieve its own emancipation. While they would be supported in this job by people from every section of society, nobody could do it for them.[35]

This gap between Marx and the 'Marxists' is inseparable from another. When Plekhanov drafted the Party Programme, he brought Marx's formula 'dictatorship of the proletariat' into it. But the Russian 'Marxists' read this phrase quite differently from anything Marx would have recognised.

Marx and Engels used the term precisely to distinguish themselves from the followers of the French revolutionary Auguste Blanqui (1805–1881). Blanqui spent his life plotting for a revolutionary 'dictatorship', to be exercised by a conspiratorial elite. The workers would hear about it later. In direct opposition to this, Marx and Engels argued that communism could only come about through the action of *the entire class of proletar-*

ians, which in advanced countries was the mass of society. The state which oppressed the exploited on behalf of the exploiters would be destroyed and replaced, not by a new, 'workers' state', but by a body which would at once begin to dissolve itself into the community. This is what Marx called 'the dictatorship of the proletariat'.

But the Russian revolutionaries, with the heroic tradition of 'terrorism' behind them, had to work illegally to organise a proletariat which was a small minority in an overwhelmingly peasant country. That is how 'dictatorship' to the Russian social democrats came to mean a form of state, whose apparatus was 'unrestricted by laws'. It is clear that Plekhanov, at any rate, thought in terms of this apparatus in the hands of a determined and benevolent minority. In 1902–3, the implications of this outlook were only beginning to be discussed.

The Second Congress of the RSDLP took place in 1903, only a few months after the editorial board of the newspaper *Iskra* – which included Plekhanov, Julius Martov (1873–1923) and Trotsky – had issued Lenin's book. Lenin's formulations in *What is to be Done?* were challenged. Instead of defending them literally, he declared:

> Obviously, an episode in the struggle against economism has here been confused with a principled presentation of a major theoretical question, namely the formation of an ideology. ... We all know that the 'economists' bent the stick in one direction. In order to straighten the stick it was necessary to bend it in the other direction, and that is what I did.[36]

But by the end of the 1920s, a god-like Lenin was no longer allowed to be corrected on any topic, even by himself. These particular formulations in this particular book had become enshrined as fundamental theoretical principles.

Trotsky, for one, never accepted them. But, so great was the pressure of Stalinism, that, after 1917, he never said so in anything published in his lifetime. The statement about *What is to be Done?* which appears in his unfinished biography of Stalin,[37] instead of being the starting-point for a development of understanding of the nature of revolutionary organisation, was always an embarrassment to Trotskyists. Indeed, in some Trotskyist groups, Lenin's position in *What is to be Done?* was made a fetish, central to their attitude to theory and organisation.

In the hands of the Stalinists, the idea of extreme centralism and 'revolutionary discipline' was used to justify the suppression of all criticism or even discussion. The very idea of a 'Party' was made into the fetish of fetishes, far removed from Marx's contention that the proletariat had to 'form itself into a party'.

Another episode at the 1903 Congress is also illuminating. Discussing the inclusion of the demand for universal suffrage in the Party Programme, a delegate named Posadovsky asked: 'Should all democratic principles be exclusively subordinated to the interests of our Party?'[38] To both applause and alarm, he answered his own question decisively in the affirmative. He was vigorously supported by Plekhanov:

> If the elections turned out badly for us, we should have to try to disperse the resulting parliament not after two years, but, if possible, after two weeks.
> *Applause. From some benches, hissing. Voices: 'You should not hiss!'*
> **Plekhanov**: Why not? I strongly request the comrades not to restrain themselves.[39]

Although Lenin did not actually speak in this discussion, he was completely united with Plekhanov. As the split in the *Iskra* group revealed itself, Lenin and Plekhanov were at first lined up against Martov and Trotsky. Only in the following year did the division between 'Bolshevism' and 'Menshevism' begin to take its later shape, with Plekhanov as a leader of Menshevism and Trotsky outside both groups. (Plekhanov only began to criticise *What is to be Done?* three years after it had appeared.) Each faction, Mensheviks and Bolsheviks, adopted both the centralised form of organisation and Plekhanov's 'dictatorship of the proletariat' conception.

It is worth contrasting the views of Plekhanov and Lenin at that time with those of Rosa Luxemburg. Following the 1905 Revolution in Russia, she had intervened in the discussion raging in the German Social Democratic Party with her pamphlet *The Mass Strike, the Political Party and the Trade Unions*.

> The revolution, even when the proletariat, with the Social Democrats at their head, appear in the leading role, is not a manoeuvre of the proletariat in the open field, but a fight in the midst of the incessant crashing, displacing and crumbling of the social foundation. In short, in the mass strikes in Russia, spontaneity plays such a predominant part, not because the Russian proletariat are 'uneducated', but because revolutions do not allow anyone to play the schoolmaster with them.

'Dialectical Materialism'
The Stalinist movement has ensured that the phrase 'dialectical materialism' is widely associated with Karl Marx. It had been used earlier, but not in Marx's lifetime. In the preface to his 1908 book *Materialism and*

Empirio-Criticism, Lenin declared: 'Marx and Engels scores of times termed their philosophical views dialectical materialism.'[40] He was so sure about this, that he felt no need to give any references.

In fact, there is not one! Marx never employed the phrase in any of his writings. The term 'dialectical materialism' was introduced in 1891 by Plekhanov, in an article in Kautsky's *Neue Zeit*.[41] He thought – wrongly, I believe – that he was merely adapting it from Engels's usage in *Anti-Dühring* and *Ludwig Feuerbach*. This was not just a matter of terminology. He was intent on combating the tendency of the populists (*'narodniki'*) to put subjective revolutionary will at the foundation of their idea of the Russian Revolution. In its place, Plekhanov installed a materialism which left no room for will at all and this is what he foisted on to Marx. Many years later (1920), Lenin wrote: 'Bolshevism arose in 1903 on a very firm foundation of Marxist theory.'[42] Alas, it did nothing of the kind.

Alexander Bogdanov (1873–1928) was one of Lenin's closest collaborators and an enthusiastic advocate of the basic ideas of *What is to be Done?* Along with other Party members, Bogdanov was also an enthusiastic follower of Ernst Mach (1838–1916) a leading Austrian physicist, philosopher and historian of science, who was concerned with the methodological problems arising from contemporary developments in physics. Bogdanov thought that his ideas offered a 'scientific' alternative to 'dialectics' as a foundation for socialism.

Mach's 'theory of knowledge' was based on sensation – something like the scepticism of the eighteenth-century Scot, David Hume. Lenin, following Plekhanov, later came to see it as an attack on 'Marxist orthodoxy'. This, they believed, was founded on 'materialism', which began with the objective existence of the world, independent of what anyone thinks about it.

But that came later. Trotsky recalls how, when he came to London in 1902 (after his escape from Siberia), he told Lenin about his discussions in prison:

> In philosophy we had been much impressed with Bogdanov's book, which combined Marxism with the theory of knowledge put forward by Mach and Avenarius. Lenin also thought, at the time, that Bogdanov's theories were right. 'I am not a philosopher,' he said with a slightly timorous expression, 'but Plekhanov denounces Bogdanov's philosophy as a disguised sort of idealism'. A few years later, Lenin dedicated a big volume to the discussion of Mach and Avenarius; his

criticism of their theories was fundamentally identical with that voiced by Plekhanov.[43]

Between 1904 and 1906, Bogdanov's three-volume *Empirio-Monism* appeared in Moscow, while its author remained Lenin's second-in-command in the Bolshevik faction. After the defeat of the 1905 uprising, all factions of the RSDLP inevitably faced great political difficulties. One expression of these was the renewal of interest in Mach's philosophy of science. (Another was the effort of Lunacharsky (1875–1933) to build a secular 'socialist religion'.)

In 1905, Mach's *Knowledge and Error* had appeared. The following year, Machist members of both Menshevik and Bolshevik factions combined to issue *Studies in the Philosophy of Marxism*. In 1908, a Russian edition of Mach's earlier *The Analysis of Sensations* appeared, with an enthusiastic introduction by Bogdanov. Lenin now decided that these ideas represented a fundamental attack on Marxism and were thus embarrassing for the Bolshevik faction.

For a long time, he held his tongue to avoid a split among the Bolsheviks, and stood by an agreement on the editorial board of the Bolshevik newspaper *Proletary* that it should remain neutral on philosophical issues. Plekhanov, now leading Lenin's Menshevik opponents, was delighted at Lenin's embarrassment. He made the most of the accusation that Lenin's group were 'subjectivists' like old *narodnik* terrorists. Attacking 'Lenin and the Nietzscheans and Machists who surround him', Plekhanov gleefully alleged that those who 'talk about the *seizure of power* by the Social-Democrats in the now impending *bourgeois revolution* … are returning to the political standpoint of the late "*Narodnaya Volya* trend"'.[44]

For a time a perplexed Lenin considered proposing a struggle jointly with Plekhanov against both Menshevik and Bolshevik Machists. Then Lenin broke the agreement with the Bolshevik Machists, with whom he now had important political disagreements. Borrowing a large number of books on philosophy from the Menshevik-Machist Valentinov (1890–1975) – one of the targets for his attack – Lenin began work on *Materialism and Empirio-Criticism*, and spent the best part of 1908 on it, in Geneva, London and Paris. (Valentinov reports that Lenin returned all his books when the job was done.) Under Stalin, this book became the unquestionable source for 'dialectical materialism'.

In *The Development of the Monist View of History* (1894), Plekhanov had been rather cautious. The Machist controversy had not yet begun and 'revisionism' had not yet shown its hand.

Materialism … tries to explain psychic phenomena by these or those
qualities of *matter*, by this or that organization of the human, or in
more general terms, of the animal body. … That is all that can be said
about materialism in general.[45]

In the preface to his *Essays on the History of Materialism* (1896),
Plekhanov had brushed aside all questions about the 'theory of
knowledge':

Since I do not number myself among the adherents of the theoretico-
scholasticism that is such vogue today, I have had no intention of
dwelling on this absolutely secondary question.[46]

But in 1908, Plekhanov answered an open challenge from Bogdanov
with his booklet *Materialismus Militans*. In his usual lofty manner, he
attacked the superficiality of Bogdanov's arguments. For Plekhanov and
Lenin, the way to combat philosophical attacks on Marxism in the International was to underline the continuity between the views of Marx and
Engels and those of earlier materialists, and they both thought this
meant stressing how 'materialist' they were. So, in *Materialismus Militans*,
Plekhanov gave a 'definition of matter':

In contrast to 'spirit', we call 'matter' that which acts on our sense-
organs and arouses in us various sensations. … We call material
objects (bodies) those objects that exist independently of our consciousness and, acting on our senses, arouse in us certain *sensations*
which in turn underlie our notions of the material world, that is, of
those same material objects as well as of their reciprocal relationships.[47]

Plekhanov goes on to identify matter with Kant's 'things-in-
themselves', while denying Kant's contention that 'things-in-themselves'
were essentially unknowable. Does that mean that our sensations give
us direct knowledge of matter? No, says Plekhanov. What we get
from our senses is a 'hieroglyph', which has then to be decoded by
thought.

Plekhanov's 'definition' of matter has an honourable history, but not
in the works of either Marx or Engels. That matter is 'given to us in
our sensations' had certainly been the view of the old materialists,
whose writings were well known to Plekhanov. He quotes the great
eighteenth-century mechanical materialist Holbach, for whom 'matter
is what acts in one way or another on our senses'.[48]

But these were bourgeois thinkers, in the sense that they took human
beings to be discrete, reasoning atoms. For them, sensations were the

physical traces left by the impact of external bodies in these individuals. Knowledge was thus implicitly reducible to the passive responses of individual citizens, who were assumed to exist outside society.[49]

Plekhanov had tried to demonstrate that Bernstein's return to Kant (or rather to the neo-Kantian version of Kant) was part of a general adaptation to bourgeois society. But, in effect, so was his version of eighteenth-century materialism. In *Materialism and Empirio-Criticism*, Lenin also gives a definition of matter, very much like Plekhanov's:

> Matter is a philosophical category denoting the objective reality which is given to man by his sensations, and which is copied, photographed and reflected by our sensations while existing independently of them.[50]

Characteristically, to show that he is a more radical philosopher than Plekhanov, Lenin sharpens his materialism. He insists that sensations are 'copies' of material reality. The theory of 'hieroglyphs', declares Lenin, is an impermissible concession to the Kantians and positivists: 'To regard our sensations as images of the external world, to recognise objective truth, to hold the materialist theory of knowledge – these are all one and the same thing.'[51] (By the way, Plekhanov later withdrew his use of the term 'hieroglyph', saying it had been 'a mistake'.)

Lenin's 'copy theory' – and it is hard to see just what he meant by it – was designed to root out the last traces of idealism and subjectivism. But, in fact, it left 'dialectical materialism' perched precariously on the view that 'objective truth' is founded on individual 'sensation'.

In *Materialism and Empirio-Criticism*, Lenin is sometimes vaguely aware of these weaknesses, but on the fundamental issues he is still not able to break free from Plekhanov's philosophical tutelage. When, twenty years later, Lenin's works had been transformed from a living struggle for clarification into religious dogma, this provided a basis for the philosophy of the bureaucrats.

Lenin did emphasise Engels's remark in *Ludwig Feuerbach* that materialism 'has to change its form' 'with every epoch-making discovery even in the sphere of natural science'. But *Materialism and Empirio-Criticism*, with all its inconsistencies, itself became fixed as a definitive text, a central part of the canon of 'dialectical materialism'. This dogmatic outlook was, of course, obligatory for Stalinists; but those who followed Trotsky in his battle against Stalinism were never able to challenge it and so free themselves from its influence.

Lenin's political conceptions were demonstrated in practice to be diametrically opposed to those of his philosophical mentor. But he was never able to clarify the philosophical foundation of this vital difference, or his attitude to Plekhanov's work as a whole. While denouncing Plekhanov's political treachery in 1905, his attitude to the World War in 1914 and his support for Kerensky's Provisional Government in 1917, he never ceased to pay tribute to Plekhanov's philosophical work and never broke with it openly. (Interestingly, Bogdanov's views actually crop up again in the history of Bolshevism, through their influence on Bukharin.)

Lenin versus 'Orthodoxy'

Until August 1914, Lenin supported the theoretical authority of Karl Kautsky without fundamental disagreement. Although the Bolsheviks had fought against Georgi Plekhanov's political line for a decade, his writings on philosophy continued to be accepted by them as the genuine continuation of the work of Marx and Engels, with only minor amendments.

In the early part of the century, as the acknowledged leader of the International, Kautsky, supported by Plekhanov, had signed, and sometimes written, resolutions pledging working-class action against imperialist war. Then, in August 1914, these two became supporters of opposing empires in the imperialist war. When the German Social Democrats voted for the Kaiser's War Budget in the Reichstag, only Karl Liebknecht's voice protested. Kautsky, the 'pope of Marxism', found quotations from Marx and Engels to justify some kind of compromise. The Second International, as the universally accepted organisation of workers' parties, was finished.

This evolution of the leader of Marxist 'orthodoxy' came as no great surprise to Rosa Luxemburg. She had broken with Kautsky four years earlier, in a dispute in which Lenin had sided with Kautsky. Now, she brilliantly analysed the break-up of the International, and with her co-thinkers fought heroically to reaffirm the principles of proletarian internationalism. In 1919, she was to meet a brutal death at the hands of thugs encouraged by the Social Democratic leaders.

But to Lenin, Kautsky's 1914 betrayal was totally unexpected. Shocked by this development, he determined to discover all its implications and its objective basis. He began to probe every aspect of the ideas of the International, including especially his own – although he rarely says so.

In Switzerland at the start of the war, he turned to the study of philosophy and especially to Hegel. In his 'Notebooks' of 1914–15, it is possible to trace how this study of Hegel's *Science of Logic* and parts of his *History of Philosophy* became more and more important to him as it went on. The Stalinised version of history has naturally denied the radical nature of the shift in his thought.

In 1908, in *Materialism and Empirio-Criticism*, Lenin had defended 'orthodoxy', leaning heavily on Plekhanov's work and quoting Kautsky as an authority. But in his 1915 'Notebooks' he writes about *Capital*: 'Half a century later, none of the Marxists understood Marx!!'[52] Lenin's startlingly self-critical statement must not be dismissed as rhetoric. He was trying to use Hegel to deepen and clarify the theoretical and political break with Kautsky and Plekhanov which he belatedly recognised as essential.

'Orthodox Marxists' – myself among them! – have twisted and turned, trying to reconcile Lenin's 'Notebooks' with *Materialism and Empirio-Criticism*, written only six years earlier. Of course, it can't be done. For example, in 1908 Lenin had identified idealist philosophy with 'clerical obscurantism'. Seven years on, he wrote: 'Intelligent idealism is closer to intelligent materialism than stupid materialism.'[53] In his earlier book, his disagreements with Plekhanov were secondary. In the Notebooks he writes:

> Concerning the question of the criticism of modern Kantianism, Machism, etc.: Plekhanov criticises Kantianism (and agnosticism in general) more from a vulgar-materialist standpoint than from a dialectical-materialist standpoint, *insofar as* he merely *rejects* their views a limine [from the threshold].[54]

And yet Lenin was never able to complete his break with the philosophical ideas he had learnt from Plekhanov.

Lenin and the State
In July 1917, Lenin sent a note to Kamenev (1883–1936) which reveals a great deal about the real story of the development of Marxism:

> Comrade Kamenev, in strict confidence, if I should be killed [the Russian original actually reads more like 'bumped off', or 'done in'], I beg you to publish a notebook with the title 'Marxism and the State' (it has been left in safe keeping in Stockholm). Bound, with a blue cover. There are collected all the quotations from Marx and Engels, as well as those of Kautsky's controversy with Pannekoek. Also

a series of remarks and reviews. It has only to be edited. I think this work could be published within a week. I think it is very important, because *it isn't only Kautsky and Plekhanov who have gone off the rails* [My emphasis]. All this on one condition; that it is in strictest confidence between ourselves.[55]

When Lenin began to write up this material in *The State and Revolution* – he never finished the work – he was surprised to find how far the views of Marx and Engels had been forgotten. This was especially striking when it came to the question of the destiny of the state in the course of the transition to communism, following a proletarian revolution.

For instance, Lenin quotes, from *The Poverty of Philosophy*, Marx's statement that 'the working class ... will substitute for the old bourgeois society an association which will preclude classes and their antagonism, and there will be no more political power proper'.[56] And in the *Communist Manifesto* he finds what he ironically calls 'one of the forgotten words of Marxism':

> ... the first step in the revolution by the working class is to raise the proletariat to the position of ruling class, to win the battle of democracy. The proletariat will use its political power to wrest by degrees all capital from the bourgeoisie, to centralise all instruments of production in the hands of the state, ie, of the proletariat organised as the ruling class.[57]

It is interesting to note that, in *The State and Revolution*, Lenin is quite clear that the phrase 'dictatorship of the proletariat', which Marx and Engels used on some occasions, is equivalent precisely to this idea: that the proletariat will organise itself as the ruling class. Then, the state will begin *at once* to 'wither away'.

Lenin notes especially the development which Marx was able to make as a result of the experience of the Paris Commune of 1871. Now he could be clear that 'the precondition for any real people's revolution on the Continent' was 'no longer, as before, to transfer the bureaucratic military machine from one hand to another, but to *smash* it'.[58]

What was to replace this 'machine'? Lenin recalls that Marx saw the form of this replacement in the way the Commune organised itself.

1 The standing army was to be suppressed and replaced by 'the armed people'.
2 The people's representatives were to be elected by universal suffrage, subject to recall at any time and paid the wages of a workman. Judges were also to be elected.

3   Instead of an executive, inaccessible to electors, 'the Commune was to be a working, not a parliamentary body, executive and legislative at the same time'.

4   Local communes would take over many of the functions of the central government.[59]

When Marx spoke of the violent overthrow of the existing order and the establishment of proletarian dictatorship, this is what he had in mind. In 1917, Lenin agreed with him, seeing the Soviets of Workers' and Soldiers' Deputies as the Russian equivalent of the Commune, as 'a democratic republic of the Commune type'.[60] But, as the brutality and desperation of the wars of intervention and the Civil War swept away all such notions, these ideas were once more forgotten.

Perhaps with the exception of the *April Theses* of a few months earlier, Lenin had never written anything like *The State and Revolution*. As a follower of Plekhanov on nearly all theoretical issues, he had accepted his teacher's crude interpretation of the phrase 'dictatorship of the proletariat', which had been written into the programmes of both Menshevik and Bolshevik wings of the RSDLP. As we have seen, it was Plekhanov who introduced the notion that this 'dictatorship' was to be exercised by a devoted minority, in a state form opposed to that of 'democracy'.

Lenin in 1914–17 was partially rediscovering Marx's notion of communism, self-critically trying to develop his ideas in the light of the collapse of the International. Returning to the most fundamental issues, he was grappling with their falsification in the movement of which he had been a part. These books are permeated with this deeper understanding of the way forward for humanity to liberate itself through the world socialist revolution. However, they represent the start of work which was never continued, and then forgotten.

Even after the political outlooks of Kautsky and Plekhanov were clear for all to see, and Lenin was engaged in defending what he thought were the ideas of Marx and Engels against them, he never published a word which challenged their *philosophical* outlooks.[61] Even when he did begin to see the importance of Hegel for Marx's thinking, and glimpsed the superficiality of Plekhanov's discussion of this, he could not break free from his mentor's influence. After 1917, there was no opportunity to continue this advance or consider its significance. Later, the mythological picture of Lenin which Stalinism inflicted on the world prevented any objective assessment being made.

Indeed, as far as I can make out, Lenin hardly breathed a word about his reading of Hegel to anyone else. I know of two exceptions. One was in the article *On the Significance of Militant Materialism* (1922), and even there, he makes a favourable mention of Plekhanov. The other reference was in the Trade Union discussion of 1920–21, mentioned on pages 31–2. There, too, Lenin was unable to talk about philosophy without invoking the name of Plekhanov.

> Let me add in parenthesis for the benefit of young Party members that you *cannot* hope to become a *real*, intelligent Communist without making a study – and I mean *study* – of all of Plekhanov's philosophical writings, because nothing better has been written on Marxism anywhere in the world.[62]

He even adds a footnote calling for a special edition of Plekhanov's works, including an index.

What I am trying to show is that the philosophical bases of Marx's thought, lost in the days of the Second International, were never redis-covered in the Third. Even before Stalin began his 'revision' of Marxism – 'not with the theoretician's pen but with the heel of the GPU'[63] – the fundamental ideas of Marx had been buried.

Engels and 'Marxism'

Frederick Engels worked closely with Marx from 1844, until Marx's death in 1883. From then until his own death in 1895, Engels was the leading figure in the rapidly growing movement which became the Second International.

It is quite common to hear Engels blamed exclusively for the vul-garisation of Marx's ideas, but I think this is too easy an option. It is true that some of Engels's formulations do lend themselves to the spread of several inadequate conceptions. In particular, the idea that *Capital* was a book about 'capitalist economics' owes more than a little to Engels's *Anti-Dühring*, his treatment of Volumes 2 and 3, and to his authorisa-tion of the appalling English translation of Volume 1.

However, compared with the later perversions of Marx's work, Engels's errors are insignificant. By the end of his life, he was almost entirely isolated amidst a sea of opportunism, and fighting a lone battle for the concepts Marx had originated, as he understood them. His followers certainly made use of the weaknesses of his writings in the con-struction of their 'Marxism'. However, in this process, these works, which played an enormous part in the popularisation of Marx's ideas, were misinterpreted nearly as badly as Marx's own writings.

Engels wrote *Anti-Dühring* in Marx's lifetime, and it rapidly became one of the most popular theoretical works in the socialist movement. (Parts were later issued as the pamphlet *Socialism, Utopian and Scientific*.) In it, he wrote: 'Marx and I were pretty well the only people to rescue conscious dialectics from German idealist philosophy and apply it in the materialist conception of nature and history.'[64]

Such remarks, made in texts designed for popular reading, do not say everything which Marx thought on these issues. But they in no way conform to the Plekhanovite picture. The closest Engels comes to speaking about 'dialectical materialism' is this:

> Old materialism looked upon all previous history as a crude heap of irrationality and violence; modern materialism sees in it the process of evolution of humanity, and aims at discovering the laws thereof. With the French of the eighteenth century, and even with Hegel, the conception obtained of nature as a whole moving in narrow circles and for ever immutable. ... Modern materialism embraces the more recent discoveries of natural science, according to which nature also has its history in time. ... In both cases, it [modern materialism] is essentially dialectic, and no longer needs any philosophy standing above the other sciences.[65]

This passage may not be written with Engels's usual clarity, but it gives no support to the idea that 'modern materialism' is just the 'old materialism' with an extra 'dialectical' flourish. Nor is there any question of 'applying' dialectic independently to nature and to history. Rather, Engels is arguing quite the opposite: the 'dialectic' of Hegel has been refounded on a materialist basis.

Engels's incomplete manuscripts on the natural sciences were written in the 1870s, but published only in 1925, under the title *Dialectics of Nature*. The 'Marxists' then absorbed them into their world-outlook. Despite the fairly tentative way that Engels wrote about the 'laws of dialectics', they were turned into tablets of stone.

In 1888, Engels wrote a review article, *Ludwig Feuerbach*, and this became another source for 'dialectical materialism'. However, it was when Plekhanov translated it into Russian, and wrote extensive explanatory notes for it, that it formed the shape in which it became a major part of the 'Marxist' canon. This is how Engels posed the question of materialism:

The great basic question of all philosophy, especially of more recent philosophy, is that concerning the relation of thinking and being. ... The answers which the philosophers gave to this question split them into two great camps. Those who asserted the primacy of spirit to nature and therefore, in the last instance, assumed world creation in one form or another – and among the philosophers, Hegel, for example, this creation often becomes still more intricate than in Christianity – comprised the camp of idealism. The others, who regarded nature as primary, belong to the various schools of materialism.[66]

Later in this book he contrasts the views of Marx and himself with those of Hegel:

It was resolved to comprehend the real world – nature and history – just as it presents itself to everyone who approaches it free from pre-conceived idealist crotchets. It was decided mercilessly to sacrifice every idealist crotchet which could not be brought into harmony with the facts conceived on their own and not in a fantastic interconnection. And materialism means nothing more than this.[67]

We comprehended the concepts in our head once more materialis-tically – as images of real things instead of regarding the real things as images of this or that stage of the absolute concept. Thus dialectics reduced itself to the science of the general laws of motion, both of the external world and of human thought – both sets of laws which are identical in substance, but differ in their expression in so far as the human mind can apply them consciously, while in nature and also up to now for the most part in human history, these laws assert themselves unconsciously, in the form of external necessity, in the midst of an endless series of seeming accidents. In this way the dialectic of ideas became merely the conscious reflection of the dialectical movement of the real world, and thus Hegel's dialectic was put on its head, or rather, from its head, on which it was standing, it was put on its feet.[68]

I do not believe that this is the same as Plekhanov's 'dialectical materi-alism' at all. For Engels, 'laws of history' have 'asserted themselves unconsciously' only 'up to now'.

In any case, Engels deserves to be considered as an independent thinker and not looked at as if his writings were merely a part of Marx's output. Since it would take me too far away from my present purpose to undertake this study here, in this book I shall restrict myself almost entirely to Marx's own writings.

Karl Marx and the Origins of 'Marxism'

'Marxism' in France and Germany
In the 1870s, socialism revived from the defeat of the Paris Commune
and the disappearance of the First International. Mass workers' organisations began to appear in many countries, often under leaderships
which tried to base their activity on what they thought were Marx's ideas.
Capital, Vol. 1, began to find a popular audience in the labour movement.

Of course, Marx and Engels welcomed such developments and
worked might and main to foster them. But they carried a price.
Opportunist tendencies, which sometimes accompanied the appearance
of parliamentary representatives of such groups and parties, were bound
up with a vulgarisation of the theory of socialism.

Marx's relations with his French 'followers' are notorious. Everyone
knows that, when he denied he was a 'Marxist', he said it in French –
and meant it. The remark was mainly directed against his future son-in-
law Paul Lafargue (1842–1911) and some of his friends. Lafargue worked
closely with Marx and Engels in building the French Party. But, while
he fervently supported Marx's basic philosophical ideas, he imagined they
had something to do with what he called 'economic materialism'.

Lafargue's political work, in the course of which he made great
sacrifices, unfortunately reflected his theory. In the early 1870s, Lafargue
tried surreptitiously to promote some kind of reconciliation between
Marx and Blanqui.[69] Later, in 1888, Engels had great difficulty prising
him away from the idea of a rapprochement between the socialists and
the demagogic proto-fascist General Boulanger.[70]

Marx and Engels themselves were particularly concerned with the
German Party, where similar tendencies appeared in the 1870s. The
problems here were bound up with the division of the labour movement
between the General German Workers' Union, founded by Ferdinand
Lassalle (1825–1864) in 1863, and the Social Democratic Workers' Party.
The latter, formed in 1869 at Eisenach by Wilhelm Liebknecht
(1826–1900) and August Bebel (1840–1913), was a section of the
International and was generally associated with Marx and Engels.

In 1875, without telling Marx and Engels and even without informing
Bebel, who was in prison, Liebknecht set up a unification of the two
groups, giving fundamental concessions of principle to the Lassalleans.
The unification Congress at Gotha set up the German Social Democratic
Party and agreed a programme which embodied many of the watchwords
of Lassalleanism.

Marx's denunciation of this document, one of his most important theoretical statements, was suppressed by the leaders of the new organisation. In 1891, Engels had still to fight Kautsky to get the fifteen-year-old *Critique of the Gotha Programme* published in *Neue Zeit*. He only succeeded after agreeing to the deletion of some of Marx's more vigorous invective. Liebknecht's *Vorwärts* – which Engels knew would never publish the document – then published a reply to the dead Marx, issued by the Party's parliamentary group.

Until the end of his life, Marx remained a bitter critic of the opportunism of the German leaders, threatening from time to time to break with them publicly. In 1879, in their so-called '*Circular Letter*', Marx and Engels mercilessly lashed the new type of 'Marxist' leadership they saw emerging. The effect of their criticism was precisely nil. After Marx's death, the German leaders' treatment of the ageing Engels was even worse. They printed his work only with opportunist omissions and amendments, and, while freely making use of his prestigious name, they effectively cut him off from the International.

Marx and the Russians

Russia has, inevitably, loomed large in this account of the development of Marxism, so it is important to clarify the relationship of Marx himself to the origins of 'Marxism' in that country. As is well known, the hostility of Marx and Engels to Russia in their earlier political work was so deep that it sometimes approached anti-Slav racism. Tsarism was seen as inspiring the most reactionary forces in Europe. (For example, Marx was convinced that Lord Palmerston was an agent of the Tsar.) Marx destested those, like A.I. Herzen (1812–1870) and M.A. Bakunin (1814–1876), who argued that there was a specific Russian national road to socialism, arising from some special qualities of the 'Russian spirit'.

When socialist ideas developed in Russia, they had nothing to do with Marx. The devoted *narodniki* were a small group of intellectuals who set themselves the task of 'going to the people' ('*narod*'). They aimed to bring about the destruction of the Tsarist autocracy and the liberation of the oppressed peasant masses. If they succeeded, they believed, Russia would never have to pass through the hell of capitalist development. To gain their goal, some of them engaged in heroic acts of violence against leading figures of the autocratic state. They hoped to destroy Tsarism by the use of the bomb and the revolver.[71]

Those, on the contrary, who thought that the development of Russian capitalism was inevitable, called themselves 'Marxists'. Russia would be forced along a similar path to that followed by countries of

Western Europe, they believed. A proletarian movement would develop in the towns and the Russian bourgeoisie would take the power in society. Organising the workers, the Marxists would be ready at some later stage to lead a socialist revolution.

But when would that be, and what would they do in the meantime? Most of the subsequent conflicts within the Russian Marxist movement were over how the struggle for socialism would relate to the democratic movement against Tsarism. In the first edition of *Capital*, in 1867, the following footnote appeared:

> If, on the European continent, influences of capitalist production which destroy the human species ... were to continue to develop hand in hand with competition in the sizes of national armies, state security issues ... etc, then rejuvenation of Europe may become possible with the use of a whip and through forced mixture with the Kalmyks, as Herzen ... has so emphatically foretold. (This gentleman with an ornate style of writing – to remark in passing – has discovered 'Russian' communism not inside Russia but instead in the work of Haxthausen, a councillor of the Prussian government.)[72]

But, unlike some of his followers, Marx was always prepared to reconsider his views in the light of new developments. As early as 11 January 1860, he had written, in a letter to Engels, about the movement among the lesser Russian nobility, concluding: 'thus the "social" movement has begun in West and East.'

A far bigger shift in his thinking was on the way. On 12 October 1868, he wrote to Kugelmann:

> A few days ago a Petersburg publisher surprised me with the news that a Russian translation of *Das Kapital* is now being printed. It is an irony of fate that the Russians whom I have fought for twenty-five years, not only in German, but in French and English, have always been my 'patrons'.

(Actually, Marx was a little too optimistic. The first translation of his book into any other language was certainly in preparation, but it did not begin to appear until March 1872, continuing in instalments until 1875.)

In 1869–70, he devoted a lot of his time to teaching himself Russian, and was soon reading Flerovsky's book on the condition of the Russian peasantry. On 12 February 1870 he wrote to Engels about it:

From his book it follows that the present conditions in Russia are no longer tenable, that the emancipation of the serfs, of course, only hastened the process of disintegration and that a frightful social revolution is now imminent.

In March, Marx could tell Engels that the colony of exiled Russian revolutionaries in Geneva had formed themselves into a section of the International, and that – to his amazement – they had asked him to be their representative on the General Council. By 1871 he was studying some of the work of Chernyshevsky on the *obshchina*, the Russian peasant commune. Ten years on, he could count 200 books in Russian on his shelves.

Following the defeat of the Paris Commune, Marx worked on the French translation of *Capital*, and on preparing the second German edition. Important changes from the first edition were introduced, and several of them concern Russia. The footnote about Herzen, quoted above, was deleted. The famous 'Afterword' to the second German edition includes a tribute to Chernyshevsky's 'masterly' work on J.S. Mill.[73] Marx goes on to refer to the Russian translation of his book, and writes at length about the helpful comments of two Russian professors, N. Sieber and I.I. Kaufman.

The German editions explain how, during the 'primitive' accumulation of capital, the expropriation of the peasants in different countries 'runs through its different phases in different orders of succession, and at different periods'.[74] In the French edition, however, Marx rewrote this paragraph to say that this 'expropriation ... has been accomplished in a final form only in England ... but all the other countries of Western Europe are going through the same movement'.[75] This limitation of the analysis in *Capital* to *Western* Europe was quite deliberate.

In 1877 war broke out between Turkey and Russia. Marx and Engels were very excited at the possibility that a defeat of the Tsar's forces would open the way for revolutionary struggles to break out. Marx writes to Sorge:

> This crisis is a new turning point for the history of Europe. Russia – I have studied the situation in this country on the basis of official and non official sources in the Russian language – has for a long period been on the brink of revolution. ... The revolution this time starts in the East, that same East which we have so far regarded as the invincible support for the reserve of counter-revolution.[76]

The victory of Russia over the Turks the following March came as a grave disappointment.

Marx was, of course, particularly concerned with the issue of land-ownership in Russia and the destiny of the communally owned peasant land, the *obshchina*, and this was also the centre of the disputes going on among the Russian socialists.

In 1877 an individual called Zhukovsky had attacked Marx in a St Petersburg journal, *Vestnik Europia (European Messenger)*, denouncing in particular that footnote reference to Herzen in the first edition of *Capital*, quoted on page 53. Sieber sprang to Marx's defence in the journal *Otechestvenniye Zapiski* ('Notes of the Fatherland'), and a comment also appeared by the editor, the *narodnik* Mikhailovsky (1842–1904). Marx drafted a reply to this latter contribution, although it seems never to have been sent.

Drawing attention to the changes he had made in the second edition of *Capital*, Marx responded sharply:

> My critic ... absolutely insists on transforming my historical sketch of the genesis of capitalism in Western Europe into a historico-philosophical theory of the general course fatally imposed on all peoples, whatever the historical circumstances in which they find themselves placed, in order to arrive at this economic formation which assures the greatest expansion of the productive forces of social labour ... But success will never come with the master-key of a general historico-philosophical theory, whose supreme virtue consists in being supra-historical.[77]

Marx and the 'Terrorists'

The illegal populist organisation *Zemlia i Volya* (Land and Freedom) had been formed in 1873. Largely consisting of intellectuals, its theoretical outlook was in no sense homogeneous. In 1879 it split and two new organisations emerged. The larger, *Narodnaya Volya* (People's Will), was responsible for renewed terrorist activity, although it did not avoid work among both the urban and rural masses.[78]

Opposing them, Russian exiles in Switzerland formed *Cherny Peredel* (Black Repartition). The '*peredeltsy*' doubted that the *obshchina* had a future, or could form the basis for Russian socialism. Instead of individual attacks on the personnel of Tsarism, they called for more work among the masses in both town and country. It was this latter group, led by the young revolutionary G. Plekhanov, which was to transform itself in 1882 into the germ of Russian 'Marxism'.[79]

However, it is here that myth and reality part company: contrary to the 'orthodox' account, Marx's sympathies were entirely with the 'terrorists'! In February 1880, Lev Hartmann (1850–1913), who had escaped from Russia following an unsuccessful attempt to blow up the Tsar's train, came to London. To the surprise of Hyndman, for one, Marx received the Russian 'terrorist' warmly and gave him every possible assistance.

In November, 1880 Marx received a letter from the Executive Committee of *Narodnaya Volya*, together with its Programme. The letter warmly praised *Capital* – 'it has become the daily reading of educated people' – and announced that Hartmann had been given the task of maintaining contact with Marx: 'We consider ourselves fortunate to have this chance of expressing to you, most esteemed citizen, the feelings of deep respect of the entire Russian social-revolutionary party.'[80]

After studying these documents, Marx ceased referring to their authors as 'the terrorist party'.

And what of the other group, the one from which Russian Marxism sprang? In a letter to Sorge in November 1880, Marx writes of them:

These persons – most (not all of them) – who left Russia *voluntarily*, constitute the so-called party of propaganda as opposed to the terrorists who risk their lives. (In order to carry on propaganda in Russia – *they move to Geneva*! What a *quid pro quo*!) These gentlemen are against all political-revolutionary action. Russia is to make a somersault into the anarchist-communist-atheist millennium! Meanwhile they are preparing for this leap with the most tedious doctrinairism, whose so-called principles are being hawked about the street ever since the late Bakunin.[81]

It appears that Marx was not clear about the political character of the Geneva group, but he certainly didn't like them.

In March 1881, *narodism* achieved its greatest success, when Tsar Alexander II was blown to pieces. Marx and Engels were delighted. When the conspirators were tried and sentenced to death, Marx was full of praise for their conduct before the court. Writing to his daughter Jenny, he declared that the defendants were 'sterling people through and through ... whose modus operandi is a specifically Russian and historically inevitable method about which there is no more need to moralise – for or against – than about the earthquake in Chios'.[82]

In stark contrast, he repeated to his daughter his opinions on Plekhanov's 'Black Repartition' group. (He was still unclear just who they were.)

The Genevans have in fact long been trying to persuade Europe that it is really *they* who direct the movement in Russia; now when this *lie*, spread by themselves, is seized upon by Bismark & Co., and becomes dangerous to them, they declare the opposite and vainly attempt to convince the world of their innocence. Actually, they are mere doctrinaires, confused anarchist socialists, and their influence on the Russian theatre of war is zero.[83]

In the same letter, by the way, Marx also gives his highly uncomplimentary opinions of Kautsky, then in London: 'He is a mediocrity, with a small-minded outlook ... he belongs by nature to the tribe of philistines.' Clearly, Karl Marx did not just disagree with the 'Marxists' – he couldn't stand them!

State and Commune

Vera Zasulich (1849–1919) was renowned as a revolutionary, honoured by socialists both for her devotion to the Revolution and her saintly character. In 1878 she had shot and wounded the St Petersburg police prefect, because he had been responsible for the flogging of a *narod*-ist prisoner. Zasulich was acquitted by the jury in a celebrated trial.[84] In February 1881 she sent Marx a famous letter. It asked for the author of *Capital* to give his opinion on the major issue dividing Russian socialists: the future of the peasant commune.

Either the rural commune, freed of exorbitant tax demands, payment to the nobility and arbitrary administration, is capable of developing in a socialist direction, that is, gradually organising its production and distribution on a collectivist basis. In this case the revolutionary socialist must devote all his energies to the liberation and development of the commune.

If however, the commune is destined to perish, all that remains for the socialist, as such, is more or less unfounded calculations as to how many decades it will take for the peasant's land to pass into the hands of the bourgeoisie, and how many centuries it will take for capitalism in Russia to reach something like the level of development already attained in Western Europe. Their task will then be to conduct propaganda solely among the urban workers, while these workers will be continually drowned in the peasant mass which, following the dissolution of the commune, will be thrown on to the streets of the large towns in search of a wage.

Nowadays, we often hear it said that the rural commune is an archaic form condemned to perish by history, scientific socialism and, in short, everything above debate. Those who preach such a view call themselves your disciples par excellence: 'Marksists'. Their strongest argument is often: 'Marx said so'.[85]

These lines read curiously, coming as they do from someone who was a close supporter of Plekhanov, the leader of these very 'Marksists', and who remained so for the rest of her life.

Marx made four long drafts for his reply, taking a great deal of trouble over them. And yet, after all his preparatory work, the reply Marx actually sent was, as he described it himself, a 'short note'. He begins by apologising for this brevity, saying that he had been ill. Our knowledge of the care he had taken over the drafts makes it look as if this illness was a diplomatic one! Another remark gives us a clue about his real political motivation: 'Some months ago, I already promised a text on the same subject to the St Petersburg Committee.'[86]

So the cool tone of his reply is explained by his preference for *Narodnaya Volya* over the group of Zasulich and Plekhanov.

Marx quotes from his cautious paragraph in the French edition of *Capital*, quoted on page 54, limiting the application of *Capital* to Western Europe. Underlining this point, Marx stresses the importance of the survival of the commune in distinguishing Russia from the Western experience:

> In the Western case, then, *one form of private property is transformed into another form of private property*. In the case of the Russian peasants, however, *their communal property*, would have to be *transformed into private property*.[87]

Finally, Marx sums up his own position:

> The analysis in *Capital* therefore provides no reasons either for or against the vitality of the Russian commune. But the special study I have made of it, including a search for original source material, has convinced me that the commune is the fulcrum for social regeneration in Russia. But in order that it might function as such, the harmful influences assailing it on all sides must first be eliminated, and it must then be assured the normal conditions for spontaneous development.[88]

The following year, when Marx was *really* ill, overcome by the death of his wife, he received a request from Lavrov for a preface for a new Russian edition of the *Communist Manifesto*. The preface was eventually drafted by Engels, but it is signed jointly by the two of them and certainly expresses the views of both. It ends by discussing the prospects for the peasant commune:

> Can the Russian *obshchina*, a form, albeit heavily eroded, of the primitive communal ownership of the land, pass directly into the higher, communist form of communal ownership? Or must it first go through the same process of dissolution which marks the West's historical development?
>
> The only possible answer to this question at the present time is the following: If the Russian revolution becomes the signal for a proletarian revolution in the West, so that the two can supplement each other, then present Russian communal land ownership can serve as a point of departure for a communist development.[89]

A year later, Karl Marx was dead.

Several aspects of Marx's views on Russia at the end of his life are important for this account. Note that in many places he stresses the role of the Tsarist *state* in the rise of capitalism and the destruction of the commune. Seeing the possibility of a Russian revolution, which would only survive in combination with the proletarian revolution in Western Europe, he emphasises the protection of the *obshchina* against this centralised state.

This emphasis should be connected with the lessons he drew from the Paris Commune. He thought it demonstrated the role of a decentralised form of political organisation in the destruction of the bourgeois state and the transition to communism. This must be underlined in view of Plekhanov's later falsification of the meaning of the phrase 'dictatorship of the proletariat'.

Also relevant here are the extensive studies Marx made in his last few years of the literature which had begun to appear on primitive societies. Among other problems, these studies centre on the way that the state came into being. (Details of this work are to be found in the so-called *Ethnological Notebooks*.[90] These were the notes used by Engels as the basis for his *Origin of the Family, Private Property and the State*.)

They are also important from another point of view. 'Marxism' made a great deal of the idea that history moved inexorably through a sequence of 'stages' of social development. This mechanical view has no basis in Marx's work, as his later ideas on Russia and on other 'precapitalist' societies confirm. We shall deal with the Preface to *The Critique of Political Economy* in more detail in Chapter 3, but for the moment let us recall what Marx wrote there – in relation, let us not forget, only to the 'prehistory of human society', not to its 'real, conscious, history': 'In broad outlines, Asiatic, ancient, feudal and modern bourgeois modes of production can be designated as epochs marking progress in the economic formation of society.'[91]

Meanwhile, in exile in Geneva, Plekhanov and his friends had formed *Osvobozhdeniye Truda* (Emancipation of Labour), the first group of Russians to proclaim themselves followers of Marx. These, the former 'Black Repartitionists' (*perdeltsy*), modelled themselves closely on the German Social Democrats, pride of the Second International.

In 1889, Plekhanov spoke at the International Workers Socialist Congress in Paris, the first major gathering of the Second International. Now beginning to be recognised as a leading theoretician of the International, he was at pains to stress the similarity between Russian and Western development.

> The old economic foundations of Russia are now undergoing a process of complete disintegration. Our village community, about which so much has been said, even in the socialist press, but which has in fact been a bulwark of Russian absolutism – this much praised community is becoming more and more an instrument of capitalist exploitation in the hands of the rich peasants, while the poor are abandoning the countryside and going to the big towns and industrial centres. ...
>
> The autocratic government is intensifying this situation with all its might and thus promoting the development of capitalism in Russia. We socialists can only be satisfied at this aspect of its activity, for it is thus preparing its own downfall.[92]

This speech helps to highlight the fundamental opposition between the conceptions of Karl Marx and those of the 'Marxists'. There is no disagreement about the historical 'facts': capital is developing fast in the domains of the Tsar; the peasant commune is being eroded; peasants are moving into the towns to work in the factories. If he had lived another few years, Marx would have agreed that the decay of this peasant basis had led to the degeneration of the *Narodnaya Voly*-ists. On the one hand, their actions had become increasingly desperate and individualist. On the other, there had grown up that 'legal populism' which later showed itself in the right wing of the Social Revolutionary Party.

But what did these 'facts' mean for Marx in his last years? What mattered for him was that an opportunity was being lost which might make the transition to communism less painful. The upheaval in Russian society implied, he thought, the possibility of imminent revolution. Russian revolutionary socialists must redouble their efforts to prepare for this revolution, while rural communal property forms still survived, otherwise this chance would not return.

And Plekhanov? As far as he was concerned, the *obshchina* was 'a bulwark of Russian absolutism', which is now 'an instrument of capitalist exploitation in the hands of the rich peasants'.[93] Neither the communal nature of this social form, nor the sufferings of the peasant masses as it disappeared, entered into his theoretical calculations. The socialist revolution is safely postponed for decades. Indeed, since even the overthrow of absolutism was to be accomplished by the Russian working class, this too was a long way off, awaiting the growth of the new class.

No wonder such views were welcomed by Kautsky. It might even be said that such people were attracted to Marx as a result of a misunderstanding. They thought that, like them, he was concerned with the 'explanation' of historical development, with 'interpreting the world' in terms of 'laws'.

They were very keen on the contrast between 'Utopian' and 'Scientific' socialism, But what they meant by 'science' was not what Marx meant at all. They thought science was about the explanation of objects from which the scientist was separated by a safe distance, and which were quite external to him. So for these 'dialectical materialists', socialism was actually a discrete mixture of Utopia and an empirical science of the 'laws of history'. From them, a bureaucratised social democracy learned to combine May Day orations about the communist future with parliamentary skullduggery.

Marx's ideas on Russia, as on many other topics, altered radically as he continually strove to deepen his understanding. Plekhanov, stressing the conflict between 'materialism' and 'the subjective method in sociology', wanted to talk 'scientifically' about the world as it existed. Marx's science started out from the 'active side', the need to 'grasp the object subjectively'.[94] For him, the point was not merely to interpret the world, but to change it.

Conclusion

We have seen that what we have been brought up to call 'Marxism' took shape only after Marx's death. In the next two chapters, we will see how directly opposed to it were the ideas of Karl Marx. How, then, should we assess the history of those Russian Marxists who fought against the opportunism of the International, breaking with it when it showed its true colours in August 1914? Did the greatness of Lenin and Trotsky really lie in their devotion to 'orthodoxy'?

I believe, on the contrary, that what is important for us today is rather their ability to break with dogma, even if only partially and unsystematically, in the course of revolutionary struggles. Where Plekhanov's 'dialectical and historical materialism' led to a fatalist acceptance that the Russian Revolution had to follow the path of the 'bourgeois revolutions' of the West, they grasped the possibility of an alternative course. (The later policies of Stalin and Bukharin, for example, in China in the 1920s, may be seen as a return to those of Plekhanov in 1905 and 1917.)

Whatever the shortcomings of their theoretical work, those who struggled for Marxism – human beings, not supermen – tried to comprehend the basis for exploitation and oppression, and to organise the working people in the struggle for their liberation. The very notion that it is possible for human beings to revolutionise the way they live was taken more seriously by these people than by anyone in history.

But such a notion raises tremendous problems, problems which subsume and transcend the work of every philosopher worthy of the name that ever lived. The energy, determination and self-sacrifice of the Marxists is a vital part of the history of our time, but it will have been wasted if we cannot look at their struggles with ruthless objectivity. Those who want to honour them must accept the task of comprehending their weaknesses.

3 'The Standpoint of Socialised Humanity'[1]

[T]he rich individuality ... is as varied and comprehensive in its production as it is in its consumption, and ... labour therefore no longer appears as labour but as the full development of activity itself, in which natural necessity has disappeared in its immediate form; because natural need has been replaced by historically produced need.[2]

Karl Marx and Humanity

How is it possible for us to grasp who we are? This, it seems to me, sums up our predicament at the end of the twentieth century. I am going to look at one side of Karl Marx's approach to this question, his conception of what humanity *is*. But Marx's conclusions cannot be separated from the way he came to them, that is, his notion of what *science* is. This will be dealt with in Chapter 4.

I contend that all of Marx's work centres on these two issues and the relation between them. He was not a sort of mental gymnast trying to find answers to hard theoretical problems. He wanted to grasp both problems and solutions in the context of the question: *what do humans have to do in order to live humanly?*

Perhaps the question can be put like this: how can humanity *make itself what it is in essence?* Marx's understanding of history, his critique of economics as a scientific expression of the existing socio–economic order, his ethical ideas, his conception of the state, class struggle and revolution, his notion of a communist society – all are based upon his way of understanding what it is to be human.

Marx did not believe that there was a *fixed, eternal* 'human nature'. So often did 'Marxists' repeat this rather obvious truth to each other that they forgot that Marx was a communist. By 'communist' I do not mean the policies, theories or action of parties or states who usurped this word. I mean that Marx concentrated all his work on the achievement of a truly human society and therefore of the notion of the truly human individual.

Of course, he knew that there was no human essence given in advance, a 'human condition' chosen for each human by God, or by the biological inheritance of *homo sapiens*. Instead, he thought that we ourselves have produced human nature, conceived as 'the ensemble of social relations'.[3] Through joint *activity*, in the course of their entire biological and social history, human individuals have made and remade themselves and their mutual relations.

Self-creativity is the specific characteristic of human beings. You might say that humans are that part of nature which is self-creating, self-conscious and social. This is not, of course, a *definition*. In fact, you cannot fit a definition – literally, placing a limit – on to something whose mode of being consists in continually making itself into something else. Moreover, as we try to examine these aspects, we will see that each is bound up with all of the others.

What can be said about something which creates its own nature? How can an individual be social? How can a part of nature be conscious, let alone be conscious of *itself*? Throughout history, philosophers have racked their brains, either trying to answer such questions, or trying to convince themselves that they don't really matter.

It is not a matter of finding a good definition in words: we 'define' ourselves – distinguish ourselves from everything else – and become conscious of ourselves as a species in the way that we live. Afterwards, some of us might try to put it into words. Marx is not concerned with finding the best theoretical distinction between ourselves and the rest of the animal kingdom. What matters is how we ourselves *act* in relation to each other and to nature, and how we can transform our way of life. What actions will enable us consciously and purposively to remake the relations between us, so that we become what we really are: all-sided, social, free individuals?

The 'Marxists' quite rightly made a great deal of the precedence Marx gave to material production in his account of human history. In *Capital*, they read:

He confronts the materials of nature as a force of nature. He sets in motion the natural forces which belong to his own body, his arms and legs, head and hands, in order to appropriate the materials of nature in a form adapted to his own needs. Through this movement he acts upon external nature and changes it, and in this way he simultaneously changes his own nature. He develops the potentialities slumbering within nature, and subjects the play of its forces to his own sovereign power.[4]

When they came to study the earlier writings, they felt quite at home with statements like this:

> Men can be distinguished from animals by consciousness, by religion or anything else you like. They themselves begin to distinguish themselves from animals as soon as they begin to *produce* their means of subsistence, a step which is conditioned by their physical organisation. By producing their means of subsistence, men are indirectly producing their means of life.[5]

Or even this:

> Natural science has invaded and transformed human life all the more *practically* through the medium of industry; and has prepared human emancipation, although its immediate effect had to be the furthering of the dehumanisation of man. *Industry* is the *actual*, historical relationship of nature, and therefore of natural science, to man. If, therefore, industry is conceived as the *exoteric* revelation of man's *essential powers*, we also gain an understanding of the *human* essence of nature or the *natural* essence of man.[6]

(By the way, before anyone objects to the apparently sexist use of the word 'man' in such passages, remember that it translates the German 'Mensch', a neutral term for 'human', i.e. the species *homo sapiens*. Indeed, Marx uses the word in the very passage where he explains the importance of the relationship between men and women: 'The direct, natural and necessary relation of person [*Mensch*] to person is the *relation of man* [*Mann*] to *woman* [*Weib*].'[7] We shall come back to this passage in a moment, because it lies at the heart of Marx's understanding of the social character of our place in nature.)

Marx is concerned with a humanity which is at all times part of nature, with

> real, corporeal *man*, man with his feet firmly on the ground, man inhaling and exhaling all the forces of nature. ...
>
> *Man* is directly a *natural being*. As a natural being and as a living natural being he is on the one hand endowed with *natural powers*, *vital powers* – he is an *active* natural being. These forces exist in him as tendencies and abilities – as *instincts*. On the other hand, as a natural, corporeal, sensuous, objective being he is a *suffering*, conditioned and limited creature, like animals and plants.[8]

We all live as part of the natural world. However much we fight to control that world, in the end we cannot evade its ways of acting. As natural beings, we have needs which spring from our natural make-up. For example, we get old and die, we have to eat and keep ourselves warm, and so on. In the process of creation and self-creation called industry, humans try to make nature work for their benefit. They succeed, but only up to a point, and sometimes the result is not what was intended.

(I remember once, when I worked in the coal industry, sitting a thousand feet underground and being told by an old man: 'Never forget: however strong the supports you set up, the roof will eventually meet the floor. Just don't be there when it happens!')

However, humanity's participation in nature is only the beginning of the story: 'Man is not merely a natural being: he is a *human* natural being. That is to say, he is a being for himself.'[9] Human production is deliberate, *purposive* activity. It involves, not only intellect and will, but also imagination. In striving to satisfy their needs, humans create things which do not exist in nature, except through their actions. Before doing something, we imagine the outcome we hope will result. In the very process of achieving the goal we have set ourselves, we begin to worry about better ways of acting and the achievement of new goals. Humans continually alter their relationships with nature and each other as they act. They develop new knowledge and new needs and find new ways to understand both the world around them and themselves.

Human creative activity involves not only consciousness, but *self*-consciousness, and that in turn is possible only in society, for nobody can be self-conscious on their own. Humans produce their own lives through the activity of the whole of society, and their *individual* relations with nature are determined by this joint activity.

The satisfaction of human needs is impossible for an isolated individual. Only by taking part in the collective production process, striving alongside everyone else to produce what we all require, can an individual become truly human. Humans are involved with the whole of nature, at every level, and that is completely tied up with our involvement with each other. Every human action, whatever it may be, is at once natural and conscious, individual and social.

The activity of labour, and the objects that result from it, thus do not just have a material, but a *social* character, belonging to the existence and the history of the whole of human society. Economics, including 'Marxist economics', which just sees their materiality, presents, at best, a flattened image of humanity.

A loaf of bread, the activity of a baker or the equipment for baking are not just material objects or processes. They are nodes in the network of social connections: the customer's relationship with the baker, the farmer who produced the wheat, the engineering worker who made the machinery, and so on. All these lives are bound together, not just by the nutritious, biological or mechanical properties of things, but by how people feel about them, about each other and about themselves.

To be human is to be both social and at the same time a particular individual, a person. Indeed, Marx's conception of communism was founded on the possibility of 'the free development of individualities'.[10] Humans do not exist as individuals outside society: 'Man becomes individualised only through the process of history.'[11] Individuality is itself produced by humans' activity in the course of their collective history.

> Man, much as he may be a *particular individual* (and it is precisely his particularity which makes him an individual, and a real *individual* social being), is just as much the *totality* – the ideal totality – the subjective existence of imagined and experienced society for itself; just as he exists in the real world both as awareness and real enjoyment of social existence, and as a totality of human manifestation of life.[12]

You are just yourself, this particular person. But that means only that you have a unique place in the world: you speak a particular language in your own inimitable manner, you like food or music of a particular sort, and so on. None of the things which make you exactly who you are exists except through the entire history of humankind.

We can be conscious of our own humanity only because, and to the extent that, we act humanly, and that means creating ourselves. We are not some kind of machine, nor are we passive victims of evolutionary history, governed by 'instincts' which can never be understood or controlled, subroutines in a universal computer program. What distinguishes humanity from the rest of nature is the conscious, *active* relationship we have with everything else, with each other and with ourselves.

Of course we have a given biological make-up, resulting from the evolutionary history of our species. This *conditions* but does not *fix* what we do, either collectively or individually. What makes us human is our conscious, social, purposively directed activity, and this produces the content of our biological form. Our relationships with nature and with each other are defined by our productive activity: we are what we do.

> The animal is immediately one with its life-activity ... Man makes his life-activity itself the subject for his will and for his consciousness.

He has conscious life-activity. Conscious life-activity distinguishes man immediately from animal life-activity.[13]

No human individual is an isolated entity, which first exists apart from everybody else and is subsequently 'moulded by society', or 'influenced by the social environment', as sociologists and psychologists like to say. Each human is – potentially – a 'social individual', and a 'universal individual'. Those creative powers which make him or her truly human, what Marx called 'productive forces', are at once totally social and totally individual. Marx takes his own work as an illustration:

> When I am active *scientifically*, etc – an activity which I can seldom perform in direct community with others – then my activity is *social*, because I perform it as a *man*. Not only is the material of my activity given to me as a social product (as is even the language in which the thinker is active): my *own* existence is social activity, and therefore, that which I make of myself, I make of myself for society and with the consciousness of myself as a social being.[14]

Anything we do is both entirely our own work, and the expression, the representation of the whole of society. Furthermore,

> man appropriates his comprehensive essence in a comprehensive manner, that is to say, as a whole man. Each of his *human* relations to the world – seeing, hearing, smelling, tasting, feeling, thinking, observing, experiencing, wanting, acting, loving – in short, all the organs of his individual being, like those organs which are directly social in their form, are in their *objective* orientation, or in their *orientation to the object*, the appropriation of the object, the appropriation of *human* reality.[15]

The human individual is *free*, self-created, but only in his or her true, social being. However, this true being can be grasped only from a particular angle, what Marx called 'the standpoint ... of human society, or of socialised humanity'.[16] And this is exactly what is concealed and twisted by the way we live.

So those forms of living which have obtained for the past few millennia, and especially for the past few centuries, are human only in a certain fashion. That is why taking the standpoint of true, that is of 'socialised', humanity is such a difficult task, accomplished only precariously, partially, in opposition to the prevailing outlook and way of life. The standpoint from which most people see the world, most of the time, is rather that of *'single individuals in civil society'*.[17] Dominated as they are by private property, money and the state, people see themselves as social fragments and society as a hostile, alien machine, a machine made up of other people.

Humanity in Inhuman Shape

An Alien World

The social form of human life in which we live sets people against each other. The social whole confronts each of us as our enemy. The whole process, both the relations between people and the relation of people to nature, is hidden, distorted and mystified. The relationship between each individual human and the society in which they live is a great problem, pondered by philosophers, psychologists and political scientists. In fact, the very existence of philosophy indicates that people do not know who they are: if they knew, there would be no need to find out.

If you look back at the history of our species over the past few millennia, and especially at our life today, the description of humanity I have suggested does not seem to fit at all. Individual lives are far from being self-created. They are governed by forces they cannot comprehend, let alone control. Their thinking takes forms which seem to be given to them from the outside. Society and nature confront them as mysterious, alien, hostile powers. People – at least, most people, most of the time – see themselves as discrete bits, colliding blindly with each other. *The way we live denies what we are.*

Because he had a conception of what was human, Marx could ask what it is to be *in*human. Marx strove to understand modern society in terms of the way the *human* was buried inside *in*humanity. He often used the metaphor of a cover or shell or integument (*Hülle*) to describe the inhuman forms which enclose the human content.[18] Liberation from these forms means to break out (*enthüllen* = reveal) of this wrapping, in which the truth lies encased (*eingehüllt* = wrapped up).

This word 'integument' is used by biologists to mean the covering round a piece of tissue. It is not like a separately manufactured container, into which the kernel may be later inserted. They belong organically together, and they have developed only in relation to each other. Both their unity and their separation belong to the essence of each, and were prepared over the whole of past history. Only humans can be inhuman. (You can't have an inhuman cat!)

Humanity has hitherto created itself encased within these inhuman forms of life, now hardened into a shell. The connections between individuals and society, between society and consciousness, between purpose and the outcome of activity, are broken and perverted and have been throughout written history. No wonder that, at this late stage of the game, the relation of humanity to nature has been completely fouled up.

Take, for example, the power of speech. It is bound up with a vital aspect of humanness: the ability of each of us to have at least some knowledge of what it is like to be someone else. Otherwise, language would be impossible. Before we can say anything, we must *know*, without even thinking about it, that somebody will hear the noise you make and understand something by it.

But look at how this ability has turned out. Today, the knowledge of what other people will make of our speech is largely the basis for knowing how to *deceive* them and make them do something they don't want to do. (Here are those 'interpersonal skills' I mentioned earlier. They are also known as 'public relations', or, in plain English, 'lying'.) 'Words were given to men to enable them to conceal their thoughts.'

To continue that passage I quoted earlier, about the relation of women and men:

> The direct, natural and necessary relation of person [*Mensch*] to person is the *relation of man (Mann)* to *woman (Weib)*. In this *natural* species-relationship man's relation to nature is immediately his relation to man, just as his relation to man is immediately his relation to nature — his own *natural* determination. In this relationship, therefore, is *sensuously manifested*, reduced to an observable *fact*, the extent to which the human essence has become nature to man, or to which nature has become the human essence of man. ... This relationship also reveals the extent to which man's *need* has become a *human* need; the extent, therefore, to which the *other* person as a person has become for him a need — the extent to which he in his individual existence is at the same time a social being.[19]

This remarkable statement brings out the unity of all of the features of humanity I have been looking at. The sexual relation is undoubtedly natural, belonging to the biological character of human life, but at the same time governed by social convention. It is as personal as anything can be, and yet it is shaped and misshaped by all kinds of social, political and economic forces. Simultaneously, it is 'instinctive', and the outcome of conscious and self-conscious decision.

That is why this freest and most human of spheres is the locus for some of the most inhuman aspects of social life. So much is this the case that Marx can make it the measure of the degree to which humans have progressed towards becoming human, social beings. I am not only referring here to the oppression of women by men, their possession as pieces of property. It is the inhumanity of human life as a whole, which conceals, poisons and perverts the true humanity of men as much as of the women they oppress.

Estranged from Ourselves

It is only too easy to see that, at the end of the twentieth century, the world is far from being a place for 'the free development of individualities'. Everything about the modern world denies and perverts what is essentially human. Social relations are fetters on the development of human creative power, colliding with it at every turn. The more this power grows, the less free our lives become and the more they are limited and poisoned.

Instead of seeing the world from 'the standpoint of socialised humanity', we look at it as isolated individuals, one-sided fragments of humanity, confronted by abstract social relations and powers. These relations are both the product of human agency and beyond human control.

We do not know who we really are, and have now almost ceased to think about what we can become. Our relations with each other are alien to us today, far more than in Marx's time. In an atomised society, individuals are not just strangers but enemies, to each other, to nature and to themselves. Human powers of creation, increased a hundredfold by the growth of technology, operate blindly against their creators and now become forces of self-destruction.

Marx did not judge such conditions against a blueprint he had devised for a 'better world'. Nor would he have accepted the view that the way we live is the inevitable expression of the way we are. Rejecting both Utopian dreaming and cynical acceptance, he decided that we live in a way which is 'estranged' from our own essential nature.

Marx reached his view of the essential nature of humanity only *through* the inhuman forms taken by human life in modern times. He saw that the forms of social life are not decided consciously by the collectivity of men and women. We create them, but they appear to be imposed upon us, confronting us like an external power, a 'second nature'.

Objects become the property of individuals, and in that form come to rule their lives. Human beings – who else? – set up and operate a political institution, the state, and it becomes a power that they have to obey. It impersonally regulates – and sometimes destroys – the lives of individual human beings. These hostile forms do not eliminate the essentially social nature of the humanity which survives inside them, but they twist it out of recognition. The problem is to grasp this human content and see the possibility of it breaking through the inhuman cover in which it has grown up.

We have seen how Marx regarded the human being: a self-creating, self-conscious and social part of nature. This conception is *at the heart* of his thinking, but it cannot be his *starting-point*. I mean that his investigation had to begin with the way we live *now*. Otherwise he would just have been a Utopian dreamer, merely counterposing an opinion about how the world *ought* to be to the way it unfortunately *is*.

Marx thought highly of some of the Utopians. People like Fourier and Robert Owen were responsible for inventing many of the ideas of socialism. They put these ideas forward as prefabricated plans for how society *ought to be*. They contended that these schemes, the result of 'scientific' work, somehow expressed human reason. But in this, they were accepting the idea of humanity as a collection of reasoning individuals, a position not all that different from those who upheld the existing social order. Thus they looked at society as if they themselves stood outside it.

While Marx took a great deal of their conception of communism from the Utopians, he rejected their basic notion of what it was:

Communism is for us not a *state of affairs* which is to be established, an *ideal* to which reality will have to adjust itself. We call communism the *real* movement which abolishes the present state of things. The conditions of this movement result from the now existing premise.[20]

The Utopian was caught up in an insoluble paradox: he was unable to explain where his own ideas came from. Consequently, however well intentioned he might have been, he inevitably regarded himself as a special kind of being, who had somehow been able to stand above the common throng.

The materialist doctrine about circumstances and education, forgets that it is men that change circumstances and that the educator himself needs educating. Hence this doctrine necessarily arrives at dividing society into two parts, one of which is superior to society, (in Robert Owen, for example). The coincidence of the changing of circumstances and of human activity or self-change can be conceived and rationally understood only as *revolutionising practice*.[21]

A lot of the confusion in the 'Marxist' tradition sprang from a refusal to think about what this meant. Ideas about 'bringing socialist consciousness into the working class from the outside', 'vanguard leadership' and so on were the result. We surely know today, and should have known before, that nobody can be forced to be free, or driven to become human. To think otherwise is to have a distorted notion of what it means to be human. Moreover, how are those who 'bring' the 'correct' consciousness to the masses supposed to have got hold of it themselves?

In a society increasingly based upon self-interest, how can anybody take 'the standpoint of socialised humanity'? Somehow, amidst all the corruption and fragmentation of the modern world, we have remained – not much, not always, generally unknown to ourselves and with many mistakes and distortions – human. At the back of our minds, we still know it.

If this were not the case, there could be no language, no science, no philosophy, no politics, no poetry, no love. These activities – twisted and perverted, organically entangled in their inhuman wrapping as they are – still do exist. That tells us that humanity does indeed survive, but bound up with, and hidden by, its direct opposite, in forms which simultaneously give us this message of humanity *and* deny it.

Thus, to the surprise of 'Marxists' and 'dialectical materialists', Marx's problem turns out to centre on the question of individual consciousness.

> Consciousness ['*das Bewusstsein*'] can never be anything else than conscious being ['*das bewusste Sein*'], and the being of men is their conscious life-process. If in all ideology men and their relations appear upside-down as in a *camera obscura*, this phenomenon arises just as much from their historical life-process as the inversion of objects on the retina does from their physical life-process.[22]

No human activity or human relationship is possible without consciousness playing a part. The fact that we go on living inhumanly shows that we look at the world in ways which make this inhumanity seem somehow 'natural' and inevitable. Inhuman forms of life cannot be seen except when wrapped up inside these forms of consciousness.

Marx was not a sociologist or an economist, nor a social scientist or political scientist of any kind, if by science we mean giving a logical account of something. For he was quite sure that the world he was trying to grasp was *not logical*. He regarded the enterprise of producing an elegant, smoothly working model of this mess as being itself an illogical dream, an attempt to rationalise the irrational.

This is how he judged the very existence of political economy as a field of investigation. It was an expression of this false way of seeing ourselves, and, through it, of the false – inhuman – way of living. So he was not trying to construct an abstract 'model' of such irrationality. He saw that this kind of attempt, which disguises inhumanity in a sort of scientific gift-wrap, is itself a symptom of a false way of life. The job of his 'science', on the contrary, was to find out how to *un*wrap inhumanity from its ideological covering. That is why a major part of his life's work was devoted to making a 'critique of political economy'.

Marx and Economics

Anyone unfortunately obliged to open a textbook on economics is confronted with masses of technical jargon, decorated with graphs and bits of algebra. Clearly, this economy thing is an extremely intricate piece of machinery, far beyond the understanding of the ordinary mortal, and its study is highly scientific. The student of economics, watching wide-eyed as this complicated equipment is demonstrated, knows that he or she is being initiated into a mysterious craft. Why should this be? Isn't the subject-matter simply about what ordinary people do almost every day of their lives? Where does the mystery come from?

Starting economics is a process of brainwashing: beginners must be taught that, if they are to complete the course and pass the exam, only *certain* questions are appropriate. Other questions, however naturally they might occur, must be sternly repressed. (Of course, it is much the same in every subject at established seats of learning. Economics is only a glaring example.)

Elementary economics textbooks like to start with helpful-sounding statements like this one (which I found in a popular textbook): 'Economics is the study of how society decides what, how and for whom to produce.' That raises more questions than it answers. Since *this* study is *not* a textbook, has no set syllabus to cover, and there is no examination at the end of it, I am free to ask some of the impermissible questions. I don't just mean issues like: Why are some people in the world very worried about their excessive food-intake, while most of the others do not know whether their children will die of starvation? Why do some people receive more money in a day than some families have to spend in an entire lifetime? Why are people out of work, when there are shortages of things they could be making?

There are left-wing economists who don't mind queries like these, answering them with a kindly indulgence. But other kinds of question are less welcome: What is meant by 'society decides'? (And what is 'society', anyway?) Why do people sell things to each other, instead of just giving them to whoever needs them? Why does most of the wealth produced by human labour take the form of *private property*, usually *belonging* to somebody who was *not* the producer? Since all economic events are examples of human action, why do we need professional help to explain them?

Given the assumptions on which their whole study is founded, it is quite natural that economists should have no patience with such queries. (It is not surprising that the last question makes them uncomfortable.) They are concerned with making a 'model' of a set of economic relationships. Before they start, they have taken for granted that the world they are 'modelling' works in a certain way. They seem to forget that they are talking about relations between and activities of human beings. So, without knowing it, they have taken a particular view of what human beings are like. For instance, they assume without question that each 'economic agent' is concerned for his or her own well-being far more than for anyone else's.

Karl Marx had a rather low opinion of economists like these, referring to them as 'vulgar'. They

> only flounder around within the apparent framework of those relations, ceaselessly ruminate on the materials long since provided by scientific political economy and seek there plausible explanations of the crudest phenomena for the domestic purposes of the bourgeoisie. Apart from this, the vulgar economists confine themselves to systematising, in a pedantic way, and proclaiming for everlasting truths, the banal and complacent notions held by the bourgeois agents of production about their own world, which is to them the best possible one.[23]

The banality and complacency of the statements of vulgar economists merely express uncritically the basic assumptions of this form of society.

Marx distinguished these people sharply from their predecessors, the 'classical political economists', a species he thought was extinct after about 1830. It included Adam Smith and David Ricardo, together with 'all the economists who, since the time of W. Petty, have investigated the real internal framework ['*innern Zusammenhang*' = inner coherence] of bourgeois relations of production'.[24] He believed these people were real scientists, however much he disagreed with their conclusions. He spent four decades working on, and never finishing, his 'critique' of political economy, including a long account of the history of the subject. What was he up to?

In the 'Marxist' tradition, it was assumed that he was trying to provide a better, 'Marxist'/socialist economics. I think this is completely false. For Marx, 'critique' did not at all mean showing that a particular set of views was wrong and replacing it with another set. He was not

interested in the straightforward rejection of the conclusions reached by
economists about the working of a mechanical system called 'capitalism'.
Nor did he follow this up by showing them how their job should really
be done. (By the way, 'capitalism' was a word Marx hardly ever used.)

Marx saw the work of the great classical political economists as
investigating the social relations of the modern world, which they
believed expressed 'human nature'. (There is an analogy with the way
Marx viewed the ideas of Hegel, which is outlined in the Appendix to
Chapter 4.) Marx's critique of political economy was his way in to the
understanding of modern social relations and an essential prerequisite
for their supersession.

What he wanted to do was to trace, in the most highly developed
work of bourgeois thought, the 'inner coherence' of the various forms
of social relations whose inhumanity had come to appear natural.
Vulgar economics was not much use for this purpose: all one can do
with it is marvel at its inanity.

But Smith, Ricardo and James Mill were tremendously helpful.
Unlike their successors, they were striving to find an objective explanation of the huge social and economic developments unfolding in
Europe during their lifetimes. What made them important for Marx was
that, when they tried to develop the 'laws of private property', they
sought to explain *rationally* what was essentially *irrational*, crazy.

Their greatest discovery was the importance of labour for the quantitative relationships between the prices of goods on the market. Marx
shows just what this means. It implies that the lives of the owners of
commodities are governed by the relations between the commodities,
objects produced by human labour. Only thus is the labour embodied
in them related to 'the collective labour of society'.

The political economists could never ask *why* the relations between
individuals took this particular form. And so their attempts to provide
scientific accounts of economic life inevitably ran into contradictions.
But that was precisely what made them important for Marx. For these
logical contradictions were symptoms of *actual* contradictions of life.
Forms of life dominated by the exchange of commodities and money
are quite crazy ('*verrückte*').[25]

> The categories of bourgeois economics consist precisely of forms of
> this kind. They are forms of thought which are socially valid, and
> therefore objective, for the relations of production belonging to this
> mode of social production.[26]

The word 'valid' – '*gültige*' – is interesting. It is used in the sense in which a railway ticket or a banknote might be acceptable. These are forms with which you have to comply if you are to participate in the existing social order. But it is a set-up which is *essentially mad*.

> These formulae, which bear the stamp of belonging to a social formation in which the process of production has mastery over man, instead of the opposite, appear to the political economists' bourgeois consciousness to be as much a self-evident and nature-imposed necessity as productive labour itself.[27]

Precisely because they strove to give a rational, scientific account of the mad world of bourgeois social relations, they pinpointed the contradictions between those relations and the true nature of humanity. So the critique of their work could take us right inside the process whereby the insanity came to seem 'natural'.

> Reflection on the forms of human life, hence also scientific analysis of those forms, takes a course directly opposite to their real development. Reflection begins *post festum* [after the event], and therefore with the results of the process of development ready to hand.[28]

Marx was not in the business of explaining the way money 'worked', but of finding out what money *was*, how this mediator between individuals took control of their lives. How did money, the global link between isolated human lives, become at the same time a barbed-wire fence between them?

> The absolute mutual dependence of individuals, who are indifferent to one another, constitutes their social connection. ... The power that each individual exercises over the activity of others or over social wealth exists in him as the owner of *exchange values*, of *money*. He carries his social power, as also his connection with society, in his pocket.[29]

Thus Marx's critique of political economy, his refusal to accept its premises while carefully tracing where they lead, gets to the heart of the problems of the modern world.

In tracing the insane 'logic' which led from the 'commodity-form' to the 'money-form', Chapter 1 of *Capital* shows how the relations between human beings take the form of the relations between things.

> [T]he labour of the private individual manifests itself as an element of the total labour of society only through the relations which the act

of exchange establishes between the products, and, through their mediation, between the producers. To the producers, therefore, the social relations appear as what they are, ie, they do not appear as direct social relations between persons in their work, but rather as material ['*dinglich*' = thing-like] relations between persons and social relations between things.[30]

Political economy – let alone vulgar economics – takes for granted the act of exchange. What Adam Smith called a 'natural propensity' of human beings, Marx saw as essentially inhuman. From the time he began to study the subject at the end of 1843, he knew that this activity was at the heart of the heartlessness of modern life. Thus, in his *Note on James Mill* of early 1844, he shows the contrast between humanity and its inhuman cover:

> *Exchange* or *barter* is therefore the social act, the species-act, the community, the social intercourse and integration of men within *private ownership*, and therefore the external, alienated species-act. ... For this reason ... it is the opposite of the *social* relationship.[31]

The exchange relation was an 'anti-social social' relation, and so quite mad:

> As a man you have, of course, a human relation to my product: you have *need* of my product. Hence it exists for you as an object of your desire and your will. But your need, your desire, your will, are powerless as regards my production ... [They] constitute rather the *tie* which makes you dependent on me, ... the *means* for giving me power over you.[32] Our mutual recognition of the respective powers of our objects, however, is a struggle. ... If physical force cannot be used, we try to impose on each other by bluff, and the more adroit overreaches the other.[33]

This was the 'Young Marx' (he was 25). When he was twice as old, writing Chapter 2 of *Capital*, 'The Process of Exchange', his message was precisely the same:

> In order that these objects may enter into relation with each other as commodities, their guardians [Marx means their owners], must place themselves in relation to one another in such a way that the will of the one is also the will of the other, and that each appropriates the strange commodity and gives up his own, by means of a common act of will. ... The content of this juridical relation (or relation of two wills) is itself determined by the economic relation. Here the persons

exist for one another merely as representatives and hence owners, of commodities.[34]

(By the way, this passage is a direct and deliberate allusion to a passage in Hegel's *Phenomenology of Spirit*,[35] except, instead of Marx's two commodity-owners, Hegel has two 'self-consciousnesses'.)

Marx is contrasting two opposite forms. Exchanging the products of labour is indeed the most human of activities: that is how we collaborate in our shared life. But the activity of exchanging *private property* defines *inhuman* relationships. And at the end of Chapter 2 of *Capital*, discussing the origin of money, Marx writes:

> The purely atomic behaviour of men in their social production process and the objective shape taken by their own production relations, independently of their control and their conscious individual actions, appear in this: that their products take the form of commodities.[36]

Within this framework, Marx traces the way that even the most objective of economists, giving a rational, 'scientific' account of the inhumanity of modern society, fails to notice its essential madness.

The 'Marxist' myth involved the belief that Marx held a 'labour theory of value', taking it from Adam Smith and Ricardo and just polishing it up a bit. Certainly, by distinguishing between 'labour' – the activity of production – and 'labour-power' – the capacity to labour, bought by a capitalist for wages – Marx exposed the origin of surplus-value, which took the forms of profit, interest, rent, etc., and showed that 'free' wage-labour was 'wage-slavery'.

Is this a different kind of political economy, as 'Marxism' believed? Not at all. What is vital for Marx is that political economy was driven on to the rocks of logical contradiction not by some mistaken arguments, but by its inability in principle to see beyond the existing social order. Marx welcomed the theoretical inconsistencies he found in Ricardo's system because they honestly expressed actual contradictions in bourgeois society. And each of these contradictions is a result of the basic conflict between humanity and its inhuman social form, the conflict which is invisible to the eyes even of Ricardo.

When Marx explains the nature of the money-relation, he shows how it necessarily transforms itself into capital, the impersonal social power which destroys the humanity of wage-workers and their families. What start off looking like relationships of freedom and equality reveal themselves as exploitation and oppression.

Marx's book is about how this inhuman social relation, capital, produces and reproduces itself, enslaving the human beings whose life-activities and forms of consciousness are alone responsible for its existence. At each stage, he describes simultaneously the forms of this movement and the falsified, 'fetishised' way it appears to those who live within these forms. That is how he finds the meaning of the struggle of labour against capital.

On his title-page, Marx declared his subject to be 'CAPITAL: Critique of Political Economy. Volume I: Capital's Production-process', *not* 'CAPITAL: A Critical Analysis of Capitalist Production', as it said on the first English translation. The significance of this tiny difference is immense: Marx is not describing how goods are produced inside a 'capitalist system of production'.

The point is that each time a worker goes to work in a factory, what she produces is not just an item which can be used, and not just a value to be exchanged for money. It is the *capital-relationship* which has been reproduced, the relationship which separates the workers, including that very worker herself, from the conditions of production, which remain the property of the factory owner. Her own activity has resulted in something alien to her.

As Marx declares more than once, what has to be explained is not the history of how these elements came together to make production possible, but how they were separated in the first place and how the separation was reproduced. That is what forced the worker to accept the position of wage-worker and dragged her out of the house and into the factory, forcing her to spend life-activity to produce something quite indifferent to her.

> What requires explanation is not *unity* of living and active human beings with the natural, inorganic conditions of their exchange of matter with nature, and therefore their appropriation of nature; nor, of course, is this the result of an historical process. What we must explain is the *separation* between these inorganic conditions of human existence and this active being, a separation which is posited in its complete form only in the relationship between wage labour and capital.[37]

What has to be understood is not just the possibility of human creativity, but the inhuman shape into which it is twisted in bourgeois society. This is *not* economics, and certainly not political economy. It is actually its direct opposite: the attempt to *undo* the work of economists. Where economics tries to explain why things are necessarily the way they are, Marx is showing the possibility and necessity of making them different.

Marx recognised the advance in understanding brought about by the great classical political economists. But their theories – for example, the relationship between value and labour – were not *his*. Where they were trying to explain value, Marx was demanding to know *why* this relationship took its particular form and *how* it could exert its power over our lives.

> Political economy ... has never once asked why this content has assumed that particular form, that is to say, why labour is expressed in value, and why the measurement of labour by its duration is expressed in the value of its product.[38]

A few pages earlier, before he develops the *forms* of value, Marx has described his task as being 'to show the origin [*Genesis*] of this money-form'.[39] Professors of economics think what *they* have to teach their students is just 'how money works', because 'everybody knows' what money *is*.

Surplus value, as revealed in the quantitative difference between the capitalist's receipts and his outlay, is important, of course. But what really matters to Marx is the essential inhumanity of one human being selling off his or her own life-activity for money, as if it were a lump of cheese or a table. The wage relationship means that human beings are treated as if they were *things*, *means* for the self-expansion of capital, not *ends in themselves*.

The standard of living to which workers and their families are condemned, and their conditions of life and labour, are expressions of this inhuman, alien relationship they have with their own life-activity, that is, with *themselves*. Thus the 'madness' seen in the value- and money-forms now returns on a higher level.

The form of capital takes over and perverts those very characteristics which belong to the worker's humanness, her ability to create socially. It is not merely that the ability of the worker to produce is controlled by somebody else, a capitalist, or his manager, that Marx is stressing here. What he wants to bring out is that this human power appears in the form of *capital*, belongs to and is controlled by capital, an impersonal social power, of which the capitalist is merely the 'personification'.

It is controlled by *nobody in particular*. In fact, it controls everybody. That is why, when workers combine to force an improvement in their conditions of work, however mundane the immediate issue, they are implicitly fighting for their humanness against the power of capital to dehumanise them. The problem is: how to make this explicit?

The collective power of labour, its character as social labour, is therefore the *collective power* of capital. Likewise *science* and the division of labour, which appears as the division of EMPLOYMENTS and the exchange corresponding to them. All social powers of production are productive forces of capital and consequently capital itself appears as their subject.

Hence the association of the workers as it appears in the factory is not posited by them but by capital. Their combination is not *their* being but rather the *being* of capital. To the individual worker it appears fortuitous. He relates to his own association with other workers and to his cooperation with them as *alien*, as to modes of operation of capital.[40]

How is it possible for the goods that people produce, merely inanimate objects, to control their lives, for 'dead labour' to control 'living labour'? It is because these objects are not just material things, but social beings, in a world where dead social beings have power over living people. It is only through the social relations between them as commodities that their producers are related.

Marx compares this upside-down set-up, in which the products of human creation control the producers, with the world of religion, referring to it as 'the fetishism of commodities'. It appears as if gold is 'by nature' money, as if labour is 'by nature' wage-labour and as if machines are 'by nature' capital.

When Marx discusses capital, he shows how this fetishism is brought to higher and higher levels of perversity. Capital, the social relation after which he named his book, was 'value in process', a 'substance which is also subject', an active power, which necessarily grew out of money and took control of everybody's life.

In engaging in the essentially human activity called 'labour', workers are forced by the inhuman forms, money and capital, to subordinate themselves to the requirements of these forms. They are caught in the grip of capital, which makes their own activity continually produce and reproduce its hostile power over them. This antagonistic relation, that of wage-labour and capital, underlies and colours everything else about modern society.

To define capital as 'accumulated labour which serves as a means of production', as Ricardo did in *The Principles of Political Economy and Taxation*, is logically equivalent to defining a Negro slave as 'a man of the black race'. The monstrosity of this logic is obvious. Economics thinks the same way about capital.

> A Negro is a Negro. He becomes a slave in certain relations. A cotton-spinning jenny is a machine for spinning cotton. It becomes *capital* only in certain relations. Torn from these relations it is no more capital than gold is in itself money or sugar the price of sugar.[41]

What is most important about capital is its impersonal *activity*, the way that it produces and reproduces itself, 'behind the backs of the producers'. Its movement is the outcome of actions of the individuals whose lives are dominated by it. But this fact is hidden from them, from capitalists, from the workers they employ and exploit – and especially from economists. This magic power is an illusion which is not *merely* an illusion: it really *is* like that.

> A rise in the price of labour, as a consequence of the accumulation of capital, only means in fact that the length and weight of the chain that the wage-labourer has forged for himself allow it to be loosened somewhat. ... Labour-power can be sold only to the extent that it preserves and maintains the means of production as capital, reproduces its own value as capital, and provides a source of additional capital in the shape of unpaid labour.[42]

Capital is an antagonistic social form. The struggle between labourers and employers is essential to the concept of this relation. It is produced and reproduced by the wage-workers themselves as they produce commodities. That is why the entanglement of the greatest of political economists in contradictions over the nature of capital was their most important contribution to our understanding.

Wealth and Value

Marx's work on political economy centred on the contrast between two opposed forms: the alienated life-activity 'subsumed under capital', and production carried out humanly in a 'free association of producers'. This contrast is not about whether the 'same' object with the 'same' materials and equipment was being made.

That is why he stressed the opposition between *value*, a 'purely social reality', belonging only to an inhuman form of production, and *wealth*. Originally, 'wealth' meant the well-being of humanity as a whole, as in 'commonwealth'. Locked up inside the crazy, inhuman form of bourgeois property, it is expressed in quantitative terms as an amount of money. It takes the form of capital, through which the owner of capital exploits those who produce it.

In Chapter 1 of *Capital*, there are two statements within a few pages of each other, one about wealth, the other about value.

> Labour is ... not the only source of material wealth, ie of the use-values it produces. As William Petty says, labour is the father of material wealth, the earth is its mother.[43]

> The degree to which some economists are misled by the fetishism attached to the world of commodities or by the objective appearance of the social characteristics of labour [*Arbeitsbestimmungen*], is shown, among other things, by the dull and tedious dispute over the part played by nature in the formation of exchange-value. Since exchange-value is a definite social manner of expressing the labour bestowed on a thing, it can have no more natural content than has, for example, the rate of exchange.[44]

In *Grundrisse* Marx explains wealth like this:

> In fact, however, if the narrow bourgeois form is peeled off, what is wealth if not the universality of the individual's needs, capacities, enjoyments, productive forces, etc., produced in universal exchange; what is it if not the full development of human control over the forces of nature – over the forces of so-called Nature, as well as over his own nature? What is wealth if not the absolute unfolding of man's creative abilities, without any precondition other than the preceding historical development, which makes the totality of this development – ie the development of all human powers as such, not measured by any *previously given* yardstick – an end-in-itself, through which he does not reproduce himself in any specific character, but produces his totality, and does not seek to remain something he has already become, but is in the absolute movement of becoming?[45]

Later in the manuscript, Marx discusses the way that the growth of modern technology makes possible the production of human wealth, 'real wealth' [*wirkliche Reichtum*], and a truly human life, 'the free development of individualities'.[46] This is quite opposed to the inhuman form wealth assumes in bourgeois society.

When humanity is locked away inside inhumanity, what effect does this have on the prisoner?

> In the bourgeois economy – and in the epoch of production to which it corresponds – this complete unfolding of man's inner potentiality

turns into his total emptying-out. His universal objectification becomes his total alienation, and the demolition of all one-sided aims becomes the sacrifice of the [human] end-in-itself to a wholly external purpose.[47]

Adam Smith – and David Ricardo agreed with him – called 'productive' precisely that labour which produced surplus value for capital. Those who were paid out of 'revenue' they called unproductive workers. Smith was not entirely consistent on the question, but Marx condemns those second-rate economists who criticised him. Smith's strength, thought Marx, was his determined attempt to analyse a specific historical form of production.

Marx naughtily suggests two examples of the category 'unproductive labourer': a prostitute and the Pope.[48] And there are a couple of wonderful pages where Marx pretends to 'prove', using the arguments of the vulgar critics of Smith, that the criminal is a productive worker: 'The criminal produces not only crimes, but also criminal law, and with this also the professor who gives lectures on criminal law ... .'[49] He then adds to the list: police, judges, instruments of torture, perfection of banknotes, the manufacture of locks, the books of the professor, and so on!

However, the true meaning of Smith's distinction is brought out in a further illustration.

For example, Milton, who wrote *Paradise Lost* for five pounds was an *unproductive labourer*. On the other hand, the writer who turns out stuff for his publisher in factory style, is a *productive labourer*. Milton produced his *Paradise Lost* for the same reason that a silk-worm produces silk. It was an activity of *his* nature. Later, he sold the product for five pounds. But the literary proletarian of Leipzig, who fabricates books, (for example, compendia of Economics) under the direction of his publisher, is a *productive labourer*, for his product is from the outset subsumed under capital, and comes into being only for the purpose of increasing that capital.[50]

'Marxism' was so absorbed in describing the exploitation of wage-labour by capital in purely quantitative terms that it forgot that this was only one of the symptoms of the underlying disease. The wage-worker's life was increasingly 'impoverished', however much she may be paid. A life is not only assessed in terms of so many pounds per week, as a 'standard of living', although that is part of the picture, of course, but in terms of the criterion of what is truly human.

The 'general law of capitalist accumulation' expressed the nature of this social formation,

> a mode of production in which the worker exists to satisfy the need of the existing values for valorisation, as opposed to the inverse situation, in which objective wealth is there to satisfy the worker's own need for development. Just as man is governed, in religion, by the product of his own brain, so, in capitalist production, he is governed by the product of his own hand.[51]

('Valorisation', or '*Verwertung*', means the process by which capital – 'value in process' – increases its own value.)

Consider the relation between the worker and the technology with which he spends his working life. Instead of the worker using the machine, the machine uses the worker. But the machine is the expression of human power, wrapped up in the inhuman form of capital.

As Marx's analysis in *Capital* proceeds, he describes social forms which dominate human life more and more inhumanly, less and less under conscious control. Naturally, the way economists think about them is increasingly fantastic. The forms of capital all have this crazy character, springing from the fundamental madness of exchange-value. But the absurdity reaches new heights in more developed forms of the capital-relation. Take ground rent, for instance. How can you measure land, which is not produced by anybody, in terms of commodities or money?

> The proportion of one part of the surplus-value, the money-rent ... to the land is as it stands absurd and irrational; for it is incommensurable quantities which are measured against one another here, a particular use-value on the one hand, a piece of land of so and so many square feet, and value, in particular surplus-value, on the other.[52]
>
> From the standpoint of a higher socio-economic formation, the private property of particular persons in the earth will appear just as absurd as the private property of one man in other men.[53]

Near the end of Volume 3, Marx speaks of the crazy way economists look at the world, as

> the bewitched, distorted and upside-down world, haunted by Monsieur le Capital and Madame la Terre, who are at the same time social characters and things. ... Even its [classical economics'] best representatives remained more or less trapped in the world of illusion their criticism had dissolved.[54]

In more developed forms of credit there appear financial arrangements in which money seems by magic to produce more money. It seems to have this 'occult property', without any relation to production at all: 'Like the growth of trees, so the generation of money seems a property of capital in this form of money capital.'[55] And when he talks about the buying and selling of the state debt, Marx says: 'interest-bearing capital always being the mother of every insane form, so that debts, for example, can appear as commodities in the mind of the banker'.[56]

Each of the features of modern society analysed by Marx through his critique of political economy expresses the contradiction between human potential for creation and self-creation, and the inhuman denial of this potential inside which it is imprisoned and which is the essence of capital as a social power. Under this power, individuals are regarded, and sometimes regard themselves, as merely 'the personification of economic categories, the bearers [*Träger*] of particular class-relations and interests'.[57]

The conflict between the worker and capital makes this visible, palpable. The workers as a class link up with the means of production, which represent the knowledge of society as a whole, as individuals – that is, when they sell their human capacity, labour-power, in return for wages. They are thus shut out from the true characteristics of humanity – self-conscious self-creation as part of nature.

The struggle of the working class for organised unity shows the possibility and necessity of transcending these inhuman conditions of life. Those whose life-activity is the human process of interaction with nature to create wealth, fight back against their reduction to being merely 'the personification of labour-power'. This movement – whether its participants are aware of it or not – challenges the immediate power of capital over life-activity. It calls into question *all* of the ways in which human life is treated inhumanly, the many forms of inhumanity of modern society.

In present-day society, productive labour can have no other meaning but production under the dominion of capital. Productive forces can take the form only of the productive power of capital and social relations of production can only be the impersonal, abstract relations of capital. The aim of Marx's 'critique of political economy' is to exhibit and to challenge the assumption, common to all schools of economics, that there have to be social forms like these, distinct from and in opposition to the lives of the people who live within them.

What is History?
Because of our alienated lives, the historical process seems to be driven by a force external to human life, something which *happens* to us,

rather than something which we *do*. Marx insists that history is the *activity* of men and women, but they have not always got the results they expected:

> Men make their own history, but they do not make it just as they please; they do not make it under circumstances chosen by themselves, but under circumstances directly encountered, given and transmitted from the past. The tradition of all the dead generations weighs like a nightmare on the brain of the living.[58]

Of course, we can never escape from our history. It will always provide the conditions for our lives. One day, however, it will not be 'like a nightmare'.

'Marxism' read this account of the historical process as if Marx was describing an eternal and essential characteristic of human life. The whole point of his work was the exact opposite. He was talking about the inhuman condition, when our lives are steered by what seem to be external forces. 'History' appears as the active subject, and we are just its puppets, pulled around by 'historical forces'. Living *humanly* implies that the social relations between us will be subject to our collective decision. This will be the beginning of our 'real, conscious history'.

In the estranged form of life, human creative powers operate within the framework of alienated social relations, continually colliding with them. The self-activities ('*Selbstbetätigungen*') of individuals

> appear as a world for themselves, quite independent of and divorced from the individuals, alongside the individuals; the reason for this is that the individuals, whose forces they are, exist split up and in opposition to one another.[59]

For humans to be 'split up and in opposition to each other' implies they are also in opposition to themselves. To be human entails productive activity and social connection forming a united whole. At present, they directly conflict with each other. One result of this conflict is the splintering of the social totality and of individual personalities.

'Marxism' made a mechanical 'model' out of Marx's metaphor about 'basis and superstructure'. This is what Marx actually says, in the most famous statement of his thoughts on the matter, the much reprinted Preface to *A Contribution to the Critique of Political Economy*.

> The sum total of these relations of production constitutes [*bilden* = shapes, forms] the economic structure of society, the real basis, on which rises a legal and political superstructure, and to which

correspond definite [*bestimmte*] forms of social consciousness. The mode of production of material [*materiellen*] life, conditions [*bedingt*] the social, political and intellectual [*geistigen* = spiritual] life process in general.[60]

'Marxism' in its cruder forms managed to read this as a description of changes in consciousness being *caused* by the action of production relations. (Some accounts even say *productive forces*, while the worst say this just means *technology*.) Even if Marx was not sufficiently clear in this very concentrated passage, the causal interpretation cannot be right. I think he means that when our social relations are strangers to us, our enemies, we do not control our lives. Our ideas arise within forms which we do not create, given to us 'independently of our will'.

When life goes on inside a set of estranged relations, all this is concealed. The social connections appear to have a life of their own. Every change in the forces of production, say, in the efficiency of baking machinery, or of combine harvesters, will upset this network of connections, in unpredictable ways. On the new basis, political, ideological and emotional life will be affected. And none of this will be the outcome of conscious decisions by anybody.

The distinction and opposition between productive forces and social relations implies the distortion of each of the pair. Marx shows the organic connection of these two opposed categories. He sometimes speaks of the social relation, capital, as itself being a force of production.[61] Abilities to produce are not consciously directed to satisfy collective human needs. Inhuman relations between antagonistic individuals hold back and pervert the development of these abilities.

Human productive capacity, human self-creation, grows up inside inhuman social forms. With it grows the possibility for living humanly – but only the possibility, for the inhuman skin acts as a barrier to the human content. In modern times, when the antagonism is at its sharpest, it is possible for this to be recognised, and for this recognition to be made the basis for conscious action.

The 'Marxist' equation: forces of production = machines + labour power, which looks terribly 'materialist', actually exemplifies the outlook associated with estrangement. It takes for granted precisely what Marx challenges: the separation of labour from the means of labour. This corrupted account of 'Marxism' held to an 'economic determinism', in which technology, in some mysterious fashion, pushed everybody along, operating behind the back of human consciousness.

The 'Marxist' discussion of the relation between 'material social relations' and consciousness implied that it accepted their separation.

Human activity can be considered independently of consciousness and its forms only by ignoring what humanity is. When Marx said: 'It is not the consciousness of men that determines [*bestimmt*] their being but their social being that determines their consciousness',[62] the 'Marxists' heard that human thinking is inevitably moulded by external 'social conditions'. They weren't listening. Marx was pointing to the way that alienated social life appears to those who live it. Their liberation means the expansion of the power of consciousness to determine their social being.

There are exceptional times when it becomes a bit easier to gain an insight into what is happening, even if it is only a partial one. This is on those special occasions when the mismatch between the human powers of production and the existing social relations reaches a climax. Then some people can become partially conscious of the meaning of their suffering and that of others, and that this suffering expresses the stunting of their human powers. The chance that a different way of living might possibly be created peeps through the alien forms: 'Then begins an epoch of social revolution. With the change of the economic foundation, the entire immense superstructure is more or less rapidly transformed.'[63]

Marx is far from regarding such changes as if they happened mechanically. Instead of individual men and women simply obeying the dictates of History, he is concerned with what individuals think and do in such periods of change, when suffering pushes them to ask: *why*? It then might become possible for some of them to see that their misery arises from the collision between their human potential and the existing social set-up. Then they struggle to find ways to remake their social relationships.

Marx is especially keen to point out that, while 'material changes in the economic conditions of production' may be 'determined with the precision of natural science', this is by no means true of 'ideological forms' like law, politics, religion, art or philosophy. These are the forms in which 'men become conscious of this conflict and fight it out. ... This consciousness must be explained rather from the contradictions of material life.'[64]

In *Grundrisse*, there is a passage comparing the consciousness of the proletarian with that of the slave, which I think ought to make even the most hardened 'Marxist' stop and think.

> The recognition of the products as its own, and its awareness that its separation from the conditions of its realisation is improper and imposed by force, is an enormous consciousness, and is itself the

product of the mode of production based on capital, and just as much the knell to its doom as the consciousness of the slave that he cannot be the *property of another*, his consciousness of being a person, reduced slavery to an artificial lingering existence, and made it impossible for it to continue to provide the basis of production.[65]

Now look again at what Marx includes under the heading of 'super-structure' (*'Uberbau'*): law, state, religion and philosophy – all those institutions and forms of thought which characterise estrangement. Each of them has, of course, played its part in the process of history, but as a form which expresses the antagonism between individuals and society. Each of them is an inhuman, non-social form of something human and communal, a form of human life which denies humanity. This illustrates Marx's remark that our lives appear to be 'ruled by abstractions' – money, nation, state, and so on – while 'the abstraction or idea is nothing but the theoretical expression of those material relationships which dominate the individuals'.[66]

In *Grundrisse*, Marx sets out his understanding of historical necessity as something to be *overcome*. Talking about the 'distortion and inversion' involved in the exploitative relations of wage-labour and capital, Marx stresses that

> this process of inversion is merely an *historical* necessity, merely a necessity for the development of the productive forces from a definite historical point of departure, or basis. In no way is it an *absolute* necessity of production; it is, rather, a transitory [*verschwindene* = disppearing] one, and the result and immanent aim of this process is to transcend this basis itself and this form of the process.[67]

There are laws of nature: we make use of them in our work if we can, but we cannot alter them. There are laws of history: the aim is to overcome them. Marx's view of history referred to the history of humanity locked inside its inhuman shell – and its struggle to get out. Only in this context can you ask *why* this opposition exists between human productive powers and the social relations within which they develop. Only then does it make sense to ask *how* this breach can be transcended. This division is the basis for those 'contradictions of material life', which alone provide the possibility of understanding *why* forms of consciousness appear to be independent of the way we live.

Marx's conception of the historical development of estranged life thus centres on the nature of human *activity* and the growth of human *creative power*. In a society in which relations between humans is col-

lectively and consciously decided, and which thus corresponds to the
essential characteristics of humanity, Marx foresees that 'productive forces
and social relations' will be 'two sides of the development of the social
individual'.[68]

When I mentioned, on page 91, the elements which Marx included
as belonging to the 'superstructure', I omitted one from the list: art. What
is that doing alongside religion, philosophy, law and politics? I think what
it has in common with the rest is its separation from *living*, and the fact
that its practice is in the hands of special people called 'artists'.
Overcoming estrangement would involve the organic unity of artistic
production with all other departments of production. Imagination will
be united with intellect, feeling with reason.

And yet, even today, things of beauty and the modes of their
production might give us a window on to humanness, demonstrating
the possibility of free creation. Only the window is dirty, smeared
with the filth of money, oppression, exploitation and privilege, and the
vision we can sometimes discern through it is of a world mockingly inaccessible to us.

Marx understands history as a double movement. 'Humanness',
human creativity, expands with every advance of technology. But it does
so inside a progressively dehumanised cage. The conflict and organic
interdependence of these two sides is the source of change. This is the
lesson of the twentieth century, even more clearly than of the nineteenth.
In the twenty-first century, will the conditions at last exist for this contradiction to be resolved?

Class Struggle

Everybody knows the statement with which Marx and Engels began their
Communist Manifesto: 'The history of all hitherto existing society is the
history of class struggles.' However, the place of classes in Marx's view
of history is not as simple as 'Marxists' have often supposed. Even this
very sentence was not left intact: Engels later added a footnote excluding
pre-history from its scope. Furthermore, the Preface to the *Critique of
Political Economy* does not mention classes at all.

By the term 'class', Marx did not intend a sociological category, a way
of classifying people by their economic role or income bracket. It was
not a component of a 'model' of society or of history: there is no place
in Marx's thinking for that device. The classical Marxist definition of
a class as 'a group having the same relation to the means of production'
is actually one of the aspects of Ricardo's work which Marx took up
as part of his critique.

Ricardo described the division of bourgeois society into the three great classes, distinguished by their different 'revenues': capitalists received profit, workers wages and landlords rent.[69] But what Marx wants to know is how the social relation, capital, shapes our lives, and how the division into classes and sub-classes helps to hide and constrict humanity.

A class, for Marx, is a historical entity, something which *acts* and shapes itself in the course of its conflicts with other classes. The classes of modern society cannot be understood in isolation from each other. Each must be grasped in relation to the whole 'social formation' as an alienated way of living. The transcendence of estrangement implies the disappearance of classes and the antagonism between classes.

> The separate individuals form a class only insofar as they have to carry on a common battle against another class; in other respects they are on hostile terms with each other as competitors. On the other hand, the class in its turn assumes an independent existence as against the individuals, so that the latter find their conditions of life predetermined. ... This subsuming of individuals under classes cannot be abolished until a class has evolved which has no longer any particular class interest to assert against a ruling class.[70]

> The bourgeois mode of production is the last antagonistic form of the social process of production – antagonistic, not in the sense of individual antagonism, but of an antagonism that emanates from the individuals' social mode of existence.[71]

What is special about this 'bourgeois mode of production'? Why did Marx think that the modern working class was the revolutionary class, and that bourgeois society was 'the last form of servility [*die letzte Knechtschaft*] assumed by human activity'?[72] Capital produced 'the material conditions for a solution of this antagonism' in two ways. The activity of capital raised the productive power of labour. On a world scale, humanity had the potential to relieve itself of inhuman conditions of life and work. Capital perverts this potential into inhuman forms.

As it did this it produced the proletariat, a social class unlike any other in history. It was able to 'form itself into a class', to organise itself and, in the course of this activity, to become *conscious* of itself, to 'constitute itself into a party'. The inhuman conditions of life of the proletarian, the fact that she can live only by selling her human life-activity for money, means that she can assert her humanity only through the collective struggle to overthrow the power of capital on a global level.

To struggle to be human, the wage-worker cannot avoid confronting the tasks which go far beyond her individual difficulties: uniting the entire body of wage-workers, abolishing all classes, including the proletariat itself, liberating the whole of humankind from estrangement in all its forms. As a class, the proletariat had to become conscious of these objectively given tasks. It had to establish its own governmental machine, to take the means of production out of the hands of the owners of capital, and to lead the whole of society in establishing a free association of producers.

In the *Communist Manifesto*, Marx and Engels trace the historical formation of the working class as an objective process, bound up with the rise of the power of capital. The struggle for the independence of the working class begins as a blind individual struggle, develops into partial, local struggles and ends as an international fight for communism. Only when it becomes conscious of this task does its past history make sense.

The movement which begins with the assertion of the interests of individuals and of sections of the exploited class, develops into a united struggle of the entire class, first nationally and then globally, and is eventually transformed into the fight for the disappearance of all classes. The climax of this development is therefore inseparable both from the expansion of human productive power and the degree to which the movement of the working class becomes conscious of itself.

'Marxism' lost sight of the connection between class struggle and the struggle for humanity. Today, it is hard to discern this link in the activity of the labour movement. And yet, despite all the confusion and betrayal, the organisation of wage-workers into a united social power never ceases. Marx conceived of communism as the objective struggle of this movement to free itself from the alienated forms of consciousness engendered by the relations of capital. His communist political activity did not mean bringing socialist ideas into the struggle of the working class 'from the outside', but telling it, and anybody else who would listen, about the human meaning of what they were already doing.

The State – its Cause and Cure

One element of the 'superstructure' is of obvious importance. The statements of Marx and Engels about the state as an instrument for the violent suppression of the exploited class are well known. In the 1990s, we hardly need to be reminded of the brutality and corruption of those great, impersonal bureaucratic structures, the modern nation-states and the international agencies which are their globalised offspring.

But the power of the state cannot be *reduced* to instruments of violence, although these are at times its direct expression. Nor can it be understood *simply* as an instrument of the ruling class. That would be dodging much deeper questions: Why do the majority of individuals bow to the authority of the relatively small minority who exercise that power? Why do they generally accept without question the necessity for someone to govern them? To say that policemen, soldiers, judges, prison warders and executioners carry out the law neither explains why they do, nor why it is generally accepted that they should.

Our attempt to get to grips with this problem is not helped by the fact that Marx never wrote the book on the state which he had planned. The only full-length work he produced on the subject was the unfinished *Critique of Hegel's Philosophy of the State*, written (on his honeymoon!) in 1843. That was before he had started to study either socialism or political economy and before his concept of the proletariat had begun to take shape. Only the famous 'Introduction' was completed and published.

In his later political work, of course, Marx made many statements about the state and its forms – but these were never fully integrated into the main body of his work. His aim was to develop the methods with which he studied alienated economic relations in the analysis of alienated political forms.

Even the first, 'economic', part of his huge project was never completed. Its continuation would undoubtedly have dealt with the way that political forms developed historically, and with the relationship between them and the forms of consciousness in which they appear. Perhaps it would have paralleled the unfolding of the forms of value in *Capital*, Chapter 1, Section 3, and the discussion of fetishism in Section 4.

Marx spent a great deal of time studying the earliest forms of society, although only at the end of his life was there very much to be studied.[73] He wanted to understand how forms of estrangement like private property, money and the state actually originated from within social forms which had existed without them for countless centuries.

The state, like capital, finds very material and very violent expression. Yet each of them might be termed a *spiritual* entity, as inseparable from their conscious reflections as value is. It is important to distinguish between the state in this sense and its appearance in particular forms of governmental machine. Marx discusses these, the different ways that nations have been governed, and the relation between governmental institutions on the one hand, and social classes and parts of classes on the other. However, none of this is outside the framework of the basic questions: Why do some people have power over others? *Why are there states*? Why is there a split between 'civil power' and 'civil society'? These questions were central to the general issue of the relation between 'basis' and 'superstructure', discussed on pages 87–92.

Marx's battles with his main political opponents can be understood only in this context. His lifelong fights against August Blanqui and his followers, against Proudhon, against Bakunin and, before them, against Max Stirner, are fundamentally directed against the way they looked at the relations between individuals and the state. (I shall have more to say about these people when I talk about revolution in the next section, 'Transcending Estrangement'.)

Marx showed how the state, among other institutions, exemplified the estrangement of social life, the antagonism between the interest of the individual and that of the community, which is actually more basic than that between classes.

> The state is based on the contradiction between *public* and *private* life, on the contradiction between *general interests* and *private interests*.[74]

> [The community] takes on an independent form as the State, divorced from the real interests of individual and community, and at the same time as an illusory communal life. ... On the other hand, too, the *practical* struggle of these particular interests, which constantly *really* run counter to the communal and illusory interests, makes *practical* intervention and control necessary through the illusory 'general' interest in the form of the State.[75]

So the state is *a form of community*, but an *illusory* form, in contrast to the real, human community: 'In the real community the individuals obtain their freedom in and through their association.'[76]

Marx wanted to discover the basis of the illusion which is involved in this 'illusory community' and, above all, how the illusion is to be dispelled and the *true community* released.

Seen from inside estranged social forms, the state seems to speak with the voice of God Almighty, even to those of us who are quite well aware that – like the Deity – it is actually the product of the activities of all too human mortals. Explanations in terms of individual will are futile, declaring no more than that 'people behave like this because they want to'. Neither the goodwill nor the malevolence of those who control the functioning of the state apparatus provide a solution to the riddle of the state. Nor is the mystery of the state and its power explained by talking in terms of 'might': 'They would be killed if they did not obey.'

The bourgeois state, and its separation from its economic base, are shown by Marx to arise necessarily from the atomisation of individual life within that base. Estrangement and fetishism mean that the lives of individuals are controlled by powers which they themselves have made, but which lie outside themselves. Like money and capital, the political form simultaneously links people together by separating them:

> The *contradiction* between the purpose and goodwill of the adminis-tration, on the one hand, and its means and possibilities, on the other hand, cannot be abolished by the state without the latter abolishing itself, for it is *based* on this contradiction.[77]

> This occurs when matters have changed in such a way that man as an isolated individual relates only to himself, but that the means of positing himself as an isolated individual have become precisely what gives him his general and and communal character. ... In bourgeois society, eg, the worker stands there purely subjectively, without object [*objectivlos*]; but the thing which *confronts* him has become the *true community*, which he tries to make a meal of and which makes a meal of him.[78]

Take, for example, the worker who faces a new piece of technology. The law says that it does not belong to her, but to her employer. It will dominate her isolated life until either it or she is worn out. And yet it is actually her connection with the world of global technical development.

Marx saw the *necessity* of this form arising. The Enlightenment conception of pre-existing individuals freely deciding to come together to set up a state is itself an expression of the atomisation of bourgeois society. It is the illusion of 'the egoistic individual in civil society'.

However, all his needs drive him to seek out other human beings.

> Therefore, it is *natural necessity*, the *essential human properties* however estranged they may seem to be, and *interest*, that hold the members of civil society together; *civil*, not *political* life is their *real* tie. It is therefore not the *state* that holds the *atoms* of civil society together, but the fact that they are *atoms* only in *imagination*, in the *heaven* of their fancy ... not *divine egoists*, but *egoistic human beings*. Only *political superstition* still imagines that civil life must be held together by the state, whereas in reality, on the contrary, the state is held together by civil life.[79]

Society seems to be governed by rules laid down by the state. Marx shows the origin of the illusion that this is something natural. As he explained later in *Grundrisse*: 'society does not consist of individuals, but expresses the sum of the relationships and conditions in which these individuals stand to one another'.[80]

Marx sought the source of 'legal relations and political forms' in 'the material conditions of life'.

> The specific economic form in which unpaid labour is pumped out of the direct producers determines the relationship of domination and servitude, as this grows directly out of production itself and reacts back on it in turn as a determinant. On this is based the entire configuration of the economic community arising from the actual relations of production, and hence also its specific political form. It is in each case the direct relationship of the owners of the conditions of production to the immediate producers – a relationship whose particular form naturally corresponds always to a certain level of development of the type and manner of labour, and hence to its social productive power – in which we find the innermost secret, the hidden basis of the entire social edifice, and hence also the political form of the relationship of sovereignty and dependence, in short, the specific form of state in each case.[81]

Marx's analysis of commodities, money and capital showed how these social entities moved 'behind the backs' of individuals and enslaved the lives of wage-labourers and their families. So the bourgeois state, whatever its particular shape, could not but be the political representative of capital and the class of capitalists. Capital operates as a 'subject', and the state belongs in a superstructure, built upon estranged, exploitative economic relations.

Here is a quotation from *A Dissertation in the Poor Laws*, by the eighteenth-century parson-economist Townsend, as given in *Grundrisse*:

> It seems to be a law of nature that the poor should be to a certain degree improvident, that there may be always some to fulfil the most servile, the most sordid and the most ignoble offices in the community. The stock of human happiness is thereby much increased. ... Legal constraint to labour is attended with too much trouble, violence and noise, creates ill-will, etc., whereas hunger is not only a peaceable, silent unremitted pressure, but, as the most natural motive to industry and labour, it calls forth the most powerful exertion.[82]

Marx knew that, here, for 'hunger' you ought to read 'capital':

> Under capital, the *association* of the *ouvriers* is not enforced through
> direct physical force, compulsory, serf and slave labour; it is enforced
> by the circumstance that the conditions of production are alien
> property and are themselves present as *objective association*, which is the
> same as accumulation and concentration of the conditions of
> production.[83]

The way that hunger does its work, exerting its 'silent, unremitted
pressure' on the worker, is through the 'accumulation and concentration of the conditions of production' in the hands of the capitalist. The
alternative – direct state violence – would be much more 'troublesome',
as Parson Townsend's highly Christian observation correctly argued.

The state, along with religion, law and philosophy, can now be
seen as exemplifying humanity in inhuman shape. Political, legal and
scientific forms arise as illusory stand-ins for community and the
collective experience of humankind. These substitutes are necessary so
long as that experience is atomised. While we are cut off from the 'true
community', they will appear as external, enforced, superhuman powers
and our consciousness of each of them will invert their real relationship to us. Thus they accurately express the upside-down nature of the
world they seem to dominate.

They are *superstructural*, not the basic problem. They appear in history
so long as production of human life takes the form of the production,
not of the 'real wealth' of socialised humanity, but of the private
property of certain individuals. This is the basis of our dehumanised lives.
The false conceptions which accompany these forms are constituted by
our own activities, which are our own enemies.

Unlike 'Marxism', Marx himself had no notion of a 'workers' state'
replacing the bourgeois state.[84] I shall have a bit more to say about this
when I come to discuss the problem of the transition to communism
shortly. The overcoming of alienated life, what Marx called
'communism', means the disappearance of the the opposition between
political power and productive activity. Communal decision-making
becomes a part of collective productive life.

Breaking out humanity from its inhuman shell means dissolving any
political organ standing above society – the 'illusory community' – into
the 'true community'. This is the same process through which the
working class itself must disappear, along with all other classes. How
repugnant to Marx, therefore, would any idea have been that ownership
of the means of production by a bureaucratic state machine would
constitute 'socialism'.

Transcending Estrangement

Living Humanly

We often read the allegation that Marx never gave us a clear 'description of communist society'. Some people complain about this, while 'Marxism' praised Marx for it, using 'utopian' as a swear-word to put a stop to all discussion of how we should live.[85] That Marx devoted his whole life to the struggle for communism, a world in which we will transcend estranged forms of life like property, money and state, seems to be somehow 'overlooked'.

He did not envisage a process in which some experts thought up a new set of relations, which then had to be brought into being by a clever bit of 'social engineering'. The problem was how we – all of us – could break out of a shell which denies what we already are. *Collectively*, we can *remove the obstacles* to a way of life in which 'humanness', which already exists, would be allowed to develop. Instead of forcing people to live another way, the aim is to allow them to live as they truly are.

Every bit of Marx's work is based upon his conception of communist society as 'an association of free human beings, working with communal means of production, and self-consciously expending their many individual labour powers as a single social labour power'.[86]

Individuals will freely, collectively and consciously construct their social relationships. Their productive activity, instead of colliding with social relations which isolate them from each other, will be clearly seen to be *for each other*. How can the shape of such a future social form be spelled out in advance? Like this? 'From next Tuesday, you will be free, in accordance with the following rules: ....'

Marx himself described his conception of communism, before he had used the word itself, in the *Note on James Mill*, back in 1844:

> Let us suppose that we had carried out production as human beings. Each of us would have *in two ways affirmed* himself and the other person. 1) In my *production* I would have objectified my *individuality*, its *specific character*, and therefore enjoyed not only an *individual manifestation of my life* during the activity, but also when looking at the object I would have the individual pleasure of knowing my personality to be *objective, visible to the senses* and hence a power *beyond all doubt*. 2) In your enjoyment or use of my product I would have the *direct* enjoyment both of being conscious of having satisfied a *human* need by my work, that is, of having objectified *man's* essential nature, and of thus having created an object corresponding to the need of another

man's essential nature. 3) I would have been for you the *mediator* between you and the species, and therefore would become recognised and felt by you yourself as a completion of your own essential nature and as a necessary part of yourself, and consequently would know myself to be confirmed both in your thought and your love. 4) In the individual expression of my life I would have directly created your expression of your life, and therefore in my individual activity I would have directly *confirmed* and *realised* my true nature, my *human* nature, my *communal nature*.[87]

I am not going to try to summarise this amazingly rich passage, let alone the whole of this remarkable document, but here are some comments.

1 People consciously assert their individuality when they produce for each other as human individuals.
2 In this act, and in the social nature of the objects they produce, they make manifest their human character.
3 As individuals, they establish and reaffirm their social nature and their freely created social relations through the satisfaction of other people's human need.
4 In each directly communal act of production, they realise the character of everybody involved, as social individuals.

Passages like this are deeply embarrassing to 'Marxists', who ascribe such 'sentimentality' to their author's 'immaturity'. In fact, they contain the essence of all Marx's work. In my opinion, the *Note on James Mill* embodies – of course in undeveloped form – the *whole* content of *Grundrisse* and *Capital*. Fourteen years after it was written, this is how the 'mature' Marx saw it:

The bourgeois economists are so wrapped up in the notions of a definite historical stage of social development that the necessity for the *objectification* of the social powers of labour appears to them to be inseparable from the necessity for their *alienation* over against living labour. But as soon as the *immediate* character of living labour is transcended, ie its character as merely *individual*, or as only internally or only externally general, with the positing of the activity of individuals as immediately general or *social* activity, this form of alienation is stripped from the reified moments of production. Then they are posited as [social] property, as the organic social body in which the individuals reproduce themselves as individuals, but as social individuals.[88]

The belief of bourgeois economists, even the best of them, that the existing set-up is 'natural', makes it impossible for them to understand it. They are incapable of separating the social character of modern labour from its capitalist form. When this form is transcended, alienated labour – that means production in a social form which is the enemy of the producer – will be replaced with 'immediately general or social activity', in which 'social individuals' reproduce themselves and the relations between them. We shall work for each other, fulfilling each other's needs as human beings, and this will become the normal way to live and to think. Marx sees this, not as the introduction of some new, previously non-existent, social form, but as the revelation of an existing humanness which has still to shed its 'last form of servility'.

When the technology, developed inhumanly under the power of capital, is employed humanly, 'disposable time has ceased to possess an antithetical character ... necessary labour-time will be measured by the needs of the social individual ... for real wealth is the developed productive power of all individuals'.[89]

Marx's distinction between productive forces and social relations is understandable only from the standpoint of 'socialised humanity', of communism. In a world in which our individual life-activities were consciously and transparently devoted to the satisfaction of the needs of all, productive forces would be, and would be seen to be, human creative capacities, directly identified with the relations freely and openly obtaining between us. Needs, too, will become human needs, without the distortion which the market and exploitation necessarily bring about.

Let me repeat, I am not here talking about a 'blueprint for the future'. Marx's concept of communism cannot be separated from his description of the estranged life which we live today. That is why the problem of 'transition' was so badly mangled by the 'Marxists', who had forgotten what Marx was up to.

The productive powers of humanity have grown up inside the shell of inhumanity and have taken the form of means of exploitation, degradation and oppression. Simultaneously, the foundation for transcending this estrangement has been maturing. The potential for producing enough to satisfy our needs under human conditions of labour already exist. In fact, the crisis of humanity is a symptom of this possibility and its denial.

Marx's anticipation of modern industrial advance in *Grundrisse* is justly famous:

Real wealth manifests itself rather ... in the immense disproportion between the labour time employed and its product, and simultaneously in the qualitative disproportion between labour reduced to a pure abstraction and the power of the production process which it oversees. Labour no longer appears so much as included in the production process, but rather man relates himself to that process as its overseer and regulator. ... No longer does the worker interpose a modified natural object between the object and himself; now he interposes the natural process, which he transforms into an industrial one, between himself and inorganic nature, which he makes himself master of. He stands beside the production process, rather than being its main agent.[90]

Our investigations have, I hope, made it clear that this is no utopian flourish, but the essence of Marx's entire work. Modern industry, which has brought so much misery and destruction into the world, is the basis for a truly human life.

The *theft of alien labour time, which is the basis of present wealth*, appears to be a miserable foundation, compared to this newly developed one, the foundation prepared by large-scale industry itself. ... Production based upon exchange value collapses, and the immediate production process itself is stripped of the form of indigence and antagonism. Free development of individualities ... in general the reduction of the necessary labour of society to a minimum, to which corresponds the artistic, scientific, etc. development of individuals, made possible by the time set free and the means produced for all of them.[91]

Marx talked about this again near the end of Volume 3 of *Capital*.

Freedom in this sphere can consist only in this, that socialised man, the associated producers, govern the human metabolism with nature in a rational way, bringing it under their collective control, instead of being dominated by it as a blind power; and accomplishing it with the least expenditure of energy and in conditions worthy and appropriate for their human nature.[92]

It is embarrassing to read such statements in the world of the 1990s. To people living in the moral and spiritual desert of our time, how naive it sounds! Limited by the narrow horizons of the modern nightmare, they can only accept that the world has to be like it is, because that is just how human beings are. Marx's insights point the way out of this miserable narrowness. Estrangement, egoism and violent antagonism are the denial of humanity. Given the development of modern technology, only the transcendence of estrangement will establish relations which are worthy of and adequate for our human nature.

Marx, for whom communism is not a 'doctrine', but a universal *task*, anticipates a world whose social character is open, transparent, taken for granted by everybody. Relationships like this have become possible because of the growth of modern industry under the rule of capital. But that implies alterations in people, in their consciousness and self-consciousness. As the experiences of this century show, this task must raise enormous difficulties, and I don't want to pretend that Marx has answered all these problems.

What is a Revolution?

At its best, 'Marxism' thought it was engaged in the preparation of the revolutionary overthrow of capitalism, a process whose climax was to be the world-wide smashing of the bourgeois state machine. But what did *Marx* mean by revolution? Was it just a matter of a change of state form? Of getting rid of one ruling class and replacing it with another? Of altering the legal form of property?

In the light of Marx's view of humanity, we ought to look a bit deeper. First of all, we must distinguish between his understanding of the revolutions of the past — of course, he always had the French Revolution in mind — and the taking of political power by the proletariat. This is how he put it in a famous passage from the *German Ideology*:

> In all previous revolutions the mode of activity always remained unchanged and it was only a question of a different distribution of this activity, a new distribution of labour to other persons, whilst the communist revolution is directed against the hitherto existing *mode* of activity, does away with *labour*, and abolishes the rule of all classes with the classes themselves, because it is carried through by the class which no longer counts as a class, and is in itself the expression of the dissolution of all classes, nationalities, etc, within present society.[93]

(Of course, at the time when Marx wrote this, when he said 'labour' he meant 'estranged labour'.)

The problems of 'the transition to socialism', which 'Marxism' tried to theorise, still confront us. But, how can *we* — people who live as social atoms, whose lives are dominated by social relations which confront us as our enemies, whose thoughts are gripped by the power of money and the state — how can people like us think about the way to live in an association of free human beings?

Such a transformation cannot be just an updated version of the seventeenth-century upheaval in England, or of that in France at the end of the eighteenth. Those were vital experiences which involved many people – though they were still only a minority – in attempts to liberate their lives from particular forms of oppression, and to understand what they were doing. But the conditions under which they fought limited the outcome to no more than 'a question of a different distribution' of labour. I am concerned with understanding a far more drastic change.

To continue the passage from the *German Ideology*, quoted earlier:

Both for the production on a mass scale of this communist con-sciousness, and for the success of the cause itself, the alteration of men on a mass scale is necessary, an alteration which can only take place in a practical movement, a *revolution*; the revolution is necessary, therefore, not only because the *ruling* class cannot be overthrown in any other way, but also because the class *overthrowing* it can only in a revolution succeed in ridding itself of all the muck of ages [*sich den ganzen alten Dreck vom Halse zu schaffen*].[94]

This is not a change of political regime, which leaves intact the main obstacles to humanness. Marx is discussing the overcoming of centuries of alienated life. A change like that is impossible without the changing of *people* – people consciously and deliberately altering their ways of living and their ways of thinking.

Marx never altered his view that such a transformation was likely to be violent. The taking of political and social control from the old ruling class, as it clung to power and privilege, could never be an easy process. But the most changeable – self-changeable – element in the transition is the revolutionary class.

No wonder, then, that Marx and Engels could never draw a diagram showing just how it was to take place, what difficulties it would encounter, and how to overcome them. I am discussing an epoch of social development through which men and women will have to pass, and they will answer its problems in the course of creative and self-creative activity on an unprecedented scale.

The transcendence of estrangement must arise from within the old way of life, but at a particular stage in its development: the revolutionary epoch in which its estranged, inhuman character begins to impinge on the consciousness of those who live and suffer under it. Each aspect of the conflict between humanity and its inhuman shape must be brought to light, so that we can begin to see it for what it is.

Those who could grasp the general nature of the transition a bit more clearly than their fellow humans had to engage in practical activity within the conflicts in society as a whole. For this, they needed to try to illuminate each of these struggles with their understanding of the nature of their time as the epoch of the socialist revolution.

Loose talk among 'Marxists', however sincere, self-sacrificing and devoted, about a 'revolutionary party making a revolution', missed the whole point. The violence of this process, about which both we 'Marxists' and our opponents made such a fuss, is hardly the issue – there is so much violence going on anyway within our crazy world.

Marx was convinced that the transformation he anticipated would be spearheaded by 'the proletariat constituting itself as a party', supported by people from all sections of society. The idea that communists would 'seize power' and exercise a 'dictatorship' over society belonged not to Marx but to his lifelong opponent Blanqui. As I mentioned in Chapter 2, when Marx used the phrase 'dictatorship of the proletariat', that is what he meant: it was the class *en masse* which would be the 'dictator', not some self-appointed elite.

The most important feature of this class activity was that it centred on the *disappearance* of this class itself, its dissolution in the true community.

> The working class, in the course of its development, will substitute for the old civil society an association which will exclude classes and their antagonism, and there will be no more political power properly so-called, since political power is precisely the official expression of antagonism in civil society. ... It is only in an order of things in which there are no more classes that *social evolutions* will cease to be *political revolutions*.[95]

From his study of the experience of the upheavals of 1848, and of the Paris Commune in 1871, Marx clarified this conception. In *The Civil War in France* (1871), read by the General Council of the First International to its members after the brutal suppression of the world's first working-class government, the characteristics of the Commune which he highlighted demonstrate how far his ideas of transition were from the 'Marxist' caricature. The Commune was 'the direct antithesis of the Empire', 'a republic that was not only to supersede the monarchical form of government, but class rule itself'. He stressed the Commune's decision to suppress the standing army and to substitute for it 'the armed people'. He firmly applauded its democratic character, its attempt to establish a form of government in which 'the police was ... stripped of its political attributes, and turned into the responsible and at all times revocable agents of the Commune'. Among the most important features of the Commune were the efforts it made to prevent its servants from acquiring special privileges. Marx applauded the aim of setting up an 'elective, responsible and revocable' judiciary.[96]

Those who accept the 'Marxist' version of 'proletarian dictatorship' may be surprised to hear that Marx favoured the Communard notion of decentralised government, in which

> the rural communes of every district were to administer their common affairs by an assembly of delegates in the central town, and these district assemblies were again to send deputies to the national delegation in Paris, each delegate to be revocable and bound by the *mandat impératif* [formal instruction of his constituents].[97]

In *The Civil War in France*, Marx is careful never to refer to the Commune as a *state*, but as a form of government which had tried to take over the functions of the state. Indeed, in an earlier draft of the 'Address', he put it like this:

> The *Commune* – the reabsorption of the state power by society as its own living forces instead of as forces controlling and subduing it, by the popular masses themselves, forming their own force instead of the organised force of their suppression – the political form of their social emancipation, instead of the artificial force (appropriated by their oppressors) (their own force opposed to and organised against them) of society wielded for their oppression by their enemies.[98]

Considering what the Commune might have achieved, he speaks of

> all France organised into self-working and self-governing communes ... the suffrage for the national representation not a matter of sleight-of-hand for an all-powerful government, but the deliberate expression of organised communes, the state functions reduced to a few functions for general national purposes.
>
> Such is the *Commune – the political form of the social emancipation*, of the liberation of labour from the usurpations (slave-holding) of the monopolists of the means of labour, created by the labourers themselves or forming the gift of nature. As the state machinery and parliamentarism are not the real life of the ruling classes, but only the organised general organs of their dominion, so the Commune is not the social movement of the working class and therefore of a general regeneration of mankind, but the organised means of action.[99]

These words show why Marx never used the term 'workers' state', later so widely employed by 'Marxists' to describe a particular form of centralised state power.[100] When Bakunin asks, sarcastically, 'There are about 40 million Germans. Does this mean that all 40 million will be members of the government?', Marx, in 1874, answers directly: 'Certainly! For the system starts with the self-government of the communities. … When class rule has disappeared, there will be no state in the present political sense.'[101]

In his controversies with Proudhon, with Stirner and with Bakunin, what was at stake was not so much their call to 'abolish the state', but their refusal to consider what was the *basis* of the state. Only when private ownership of the means of labour, and thus the alienated form of labour, disappeared, would the state dissolve into the community. The socialist revolution was simply the way this historical process would be organised. In view of the distorting experience of the Russian Revolution, I believe these ideas of Marx are among his most relevant for our time.

Conclusion

I have reviewed some of the most important of Marx's ideas, trying to see them as revolving round his basic conception of humanity and its development within inhumanity. Does this way of looking at the world and its problems enable us to find a way forward in the next century? That is what I shall be discussing in Chapter 5.

We must get away from the false understanding of Marx as the formulator of 'iron laws' of history. On the contrary, his entire work was directed at showing that such laws can be transcended, and that humanity can take control of its own life. Indeed, that is what it means to be human.

It would be quite ridiculous to contend that Marx had a complete world outlook, or that his views formed a consistent system. His own way of thinking makes such a view quite untenable. It is not just the opinions that he held on many issues which today can be seen to have been quite wrong (I am thinking, especially, of his ideas about nationality, which are sometimes appalling); nor is it the immense size of his uncompletable project. It is because his own conception of the relation between science and the alienated social forms within which it has to develop is quite hostile to the idea of a complete body of knowledge. That is why Chapter 4 deals with Marx's idea of how knowledge developed.

4 Science and Humanity

Natural science will lose its abstractly material – or rather, its *idealistic* – tendency, and will become the basis of *human* science, as it has already become – albeit in an estranged form – the basis of actual human life. ... Natural science will in time incorporate into itself the science of man, just as the science of man will incorporate into itself natural science: there will be *one* science.[1]

Science Looking at People

Theory and Utopia

In this chapter I want to investigate the relationship between Marx's conception of science and his notion of humanity. I have argued that Marx was concerned not just with explaining the world, but with questions like these: What does it mean to be human? Why do we live in ways that deny our humanity? What must we do if we are to live humanly? After the experience of this terrible century, any attempt to get to grips with such issues is obliged to give an account of *itself*, explaining why it is the right way to go about the task. Neither natural nor 'social' science attempts this self-validation, but this was precisely what Marx wanted *his* science to do.

We 'Marxists' were keen on distinguishing 'scientific socialism' from the utopian variety. But we generally assumed that when Marx used the word 'science' he meant something like the approach of a modern natural scientist. This guaranteed, we believed, that the 'complete, integral world outlook' we called 'Marxism' was objective truth. All we had to do was to bring this truth into the minds of our fellow citizens.

Our opponents often asked us, how did *we* know this truth? If 'Marxism' was indeed a theory of history which allowed us to refer to a future situation, how could it be checked? Of course, since our interrogators were upholders of the existing social order, we could happily brush their questions aside. However, unfortunately they were not questions we ever asked *ourselves*.

I now believe these are key questions. Marx saw that humanity was trapped inside an inhuman shell. But wasn't *he* inside the shell, like everybody else? So how could he *know* about it? How could such knowledge be systematically developed, so that it could become a weapon in the hands of those social forces which were struggling to break through this shell? Insofar as we paid any attention to such questions at all, we pushed them out of the way with some arm-waving talk about 'dialectics' and a few references to 'Marx's method'. But what was this method, and why, as we used to say, was it 'correct'?

When Marx began work in the 1840s, there were already many theories of socialism and communism around. In his opinion, they had passed their sell-by date.

> Just as the *economists* are the scientific representatives of the bourgeois class, so the *socialists* and the *Communists* are the theoreticians of the proletarian class. So long as the proletariat is not yet sufficiently developed to constitute itself as a class, and consequently so long as the very struggle of the proletariat with the bourgeoisie has not yet assumed a political character, and the productive forces are not yet sufficiently developed in the bosom of the bourgeoisie itself to enable us to catch a glimpse of the material conditions necessary for the eman- cipation of the proletariat and for the formation of a new society, these theoreticians are merely the utopians who, to meet the wants of the oppressed classes, improvise systems and go in search of a regenerat- ing science. But, in the measure that history moves forward, and with it the struggle of the proletariat assumes clearer outlines, they no longer need to seek science in their minds; they have only to take note of what is happening before their eyes and to become its mouthpiece. So long as they look for science and merely make systems, so long as they are at the beginning of the struggle, they see in poverty nothing but poverty, without seeing in it the revolutionary, subversive side, which will overthrow the old society. From the moment they see this side, science, which is produced by the historical movement and associating itself consciously with it, has ceased to be doctrinaire and has become revolutionary.[2]

Marx separated himself from utopianism, which produces a pre-set agenda for human development. In doing so, he recommended a particular kind of science, one that was 'produced by the historical movement' and *knew* that it was. Only such a science can find in poverty and suffering its 'subversive side'. Its task was not to come up with a plan for a new, human, way to live and then try to get non-scientists to implement it. Rather, Marx's science seeks to remove the obstacles to a humanity which already exists. It attempts this by tracing the way that our inhuman forms of life have us in their power. But how was such a science itself able to escape from this power?

Let us look more closely at this word 'theory'. I know that Marx occasionally used the word in a general way to mean 'ideas' or 'concepts'. But I want to reserve it to mean something specific, to be contrasted with what Marx meant by 'science'. Then, I believe, I can show that, in the sense in which there are theories in physics or biology, *Marx did not have a theory*.

Theoretical science claims to have knowledge of some bit of the world, to be able to tell you what this bit is, how it functions and what it is going do next. If these claims are true, they leave no room for the selected object to choose for *itself* what it wants to do or to be, or to determine for *itself* how it relates to the rest of the universe. Thus a theory which has humanity for its subject-matter would be, from the start, denying its humanness, locking it into an inhuman prison and throwing away the key. Marx's science is the direct opposite of this notion, a critique of this kind of theory. It aims to gain systematic knowledge of the world, but knowledge which is 'in its very essence critical and revolutionary'.[3]

How to Build Yourself a Theory

In order to build yourself a theory you first need a set of *definitions*. You must know, before you can begin, exactly what object your theory is *about*. It has to be about something, to be a theory *of* something. It is necessary to fence off this 'something', draw its boundaries, make sure that it will not break out and wander all over the place.

To build a theory you also need some *categories*. These list the kinds of things you are allowed to say about the 'something' defined: how big it is, what it weighs, what it tastes like, and so on. Another requirement is a *method*. This is a pattern of procedure, a kind of all-purpose instruction manual, available for use with any kind of definitions and any set of categories which might come its way. Now you are ready to begin.

This is how natural scientists have proceeded for some time and everybody knows what a great success they have had. But even they, with a 'something' like, say, a variety of pig or a star or an atom, sometimes feel themselves in trouble at this point. First of all, whatever your 'something' may be, it has connections with other things, even with everything else in the world. Even worse, the damn thing won't stand still, and it keeps on changing into other kinds of objects which won't fit the shape of your carefully drawn boundary. You must tie it down and cut lumps off it to *make* it fit, and it might not like this treatment.

Now stand by for an important warning: when you are delimiting your 'something' in this way, putting a secure fence around it, you yourself must stay outside the fence. *On no account allow yourself to be caught inside.* Otherwise you will never move on to the next stage, actually describing the 'something' you are trying to capture, and your categories will never be taken out of their box.

Now you have new problems to worry about: having carefully separated yourself from your object, how can you get to know about it? And how can you be sure that your definitions and categories are the *right* ones? How do you know your carefully chosen method is *correct*? Where did you get it from? In order to check, you will find that you really need the very theory you set out to build.

Suppose that, when you have worked away on your defined terms, employing your toolbox of categories, according to your method, you do end up with a theory. Alas, instead of being about the world or even about a part of it, it turns out to refer only to *your own definitions*, or, as they say in the trade, it is just a 'model'.

Getting to Know Nature

I want to contrast Marx's idea of his science with what natural scientists think they are doing. Of course, I am not trying to criticise the approach of physicists to physical objects, or that of biologists to living beings. My concern is only with the way they think about *themselves* and the rest of us.

The job of the natural sciences is to systematise and expand the store of knowledge of the natural world which the human race has accumulated. In the twentieth century, technological application of this knowledge transformed every aspect of human life with breathtaking speed. Everybody knows this. But it is remarkable that only a tiny proportion of the inhabitants of the globe have more than a vague notion of what these discoveries are about. Even among this small group, few understand anything outside their own limited field of specialisation.

And what does 'understand' mean here? Most scientists just get on with their job, totally uninterested in the general meaning of their results or of the methods they used to get them. Increasingly, scientific and technical work means using tried and tested routines to answer given, partial, short-term questions.

Only rarely do those engaged in such work have the time or the inclination to think about it. Why are these particular questions being asked, rather than some others? Why have they been formulated in that particular way? What makes you think that the answers will have any value? Everybody is too busy to consider such issues, which will worry your superiors and will certainly not help anyone to get a research grant or a more lucrative appointment! Fearfully, the rest of us are obliged to leave the whole business to the experts.

The idea that scientists could take over the running of the world and organise us all on rational and hygienic lines used to be more common than it is these days. But an image of men with domed heads, gleaming white lab-coats and noble expressions still haunts us. More common nowadays is the image of the mad scientist, plotting to destroy everything.

But although most people are very vague about what scientists actually *do*, many are convinced that the natural sciences provide the model for *all* objective knowledge. The objectivity of science is supposed to result from its ability to ignore everything except the particular object under study. To get hold of systematic knowledge, enquirers must rigidly exclude themselves from the picture, along with their wishes, feelings or personalities. So studying a field *objectively*, in this use of the word, means assuming that the object's properties are quite independent of anything human and that human life is somewhere off-stage.

Of course, nobody really believes this assumption is true. Both the form and the content of each question the scientist is trying to answer has arisen out of human desires, needs, activities, history. A successful solution is one which will enable people to act upon the world in ways which are expected to change it, and at the same time transform the people involved in this task. If an object had nothing to do with us, why would we study it?

As is well known, natural science has to face some difficult questions about the consequences of applying its discoveries: the more successful they are, the more they threaten to destroy us all! Such questions are usually answered by politely referring the questioner elsewhere. They are not scientific, we are told – try Philosophy or Theology perhaps. After all, scientists add with charming modesty, we are merely scientists. We would not presume to answer problems outside our own special field.

This leads to yet another difficulty. Scientific knowledge is not just a collection of bits and pieces of information, but a systematic organisation of what is known. And yet each field of work is cut off from the totality of knowledge. This is because you are not supposed to talk about what really unites them: the development of humanity as a whole.

Each branch of knowledge operates within a given framework, a set of basic rules which has grown up over the history of the science. By definition, this framework is itself not part of the field of study. So we are rigidly limited to questions which leave these assumptions intact. The powerful attraction of this 'scientific method' is precisely its ban on self-investigation. It adheres firmly to the unanswerable logic attributed to the great Benjamin Jowett.

> There's no knowledge but I know it.
> I am Master of this College:
> What I don't know, isn't knowledge.

This way of fitting each field into its own framework, isolated both from the rest of reality and from the rest of science, is particularly suited to the application of the methods of mathematics. This has led to the notion that the most scientific of sciences are those which deal with quantity, and that real knowledge is about purely quantitative relationships, the hallmark of the *really* real. Those who think like this feel a bit uncomfortable when they hear that mathematicians are not at all sure about the foundations of mathematics itself.

Each scientific discipline – astrophysics or geology, for example – is widely supposed to provide us with an account of star-formation or continental drift, or whatever, as it actually exists. In truth, the stories they have to tell have been shaped by the presuppositions on which they are founded. Thus even the notions of space and time which they take for granted are rooted in the particular way we move about in the world, and so the particular way we live, at any particular time.

Every fundamental advance in scientific knowledge – what Kuhn called a 'paradigm-shift' – opens up these issues afresh, as if for the first time. After the shift has been completed, however, and the new way of looking at problems is accepted as the only objective one, such questions again cease to be a talking-point in respectable scientific company.

Some accounts of scientific work do not claim that it gets to grips directly with its objects. Instead, it builds a 'model' of that bit of the world it has chosen to investigate. Some elements of the model are named 'parameters'. Others are 'variables', identified with aspects of the world, generally things which can be measured or related to measurements. You can adjust the parameters until the relationships between the variables match up with analogous relationships in the world. Experimentation then means checking whether the model 'fits' properly.[4]

This method is very powerful. But what if the model, even one which shows close approximation to the world, misses aspects which are really vital? How could you detect this discrepancy? Only too often, this problem is avoided by the simple expedient of concentrating on the model and forgetting all about the world. Especially when the model is actually a set of mathematical equations, or a computer program which embodies them, the assumptions on which the whole thing is based become firmly fixed prejudices and consequently ignored. We do not even have a language in which they might be questioned.

All this is bad enough in the field of natural science, when the picture which has been distorted by this pretended 'objectivity' is one of stars, atoms or frogs. When the subject under investigation is humanity itself, the product of this way of thinking can be quite ridiculous. For the investigator is then simultaneously the investigated, and to divorce yourself from the object under investigation means divorcing yourself from yourself.

This is how it often works: the scientist is obliged to start with a particular ideological view of humans and this determines what questions he asks. Indeed, since he or she happens to be human, living at a particular time in a particular culture, how could it be otherwise? Later, they rediscover in nature the story about humanity with which their science began. An unconsidered prejudice about what humans are had been carefully buried in their scientific work, and – surprise! surprise! – they dig it up again. Their original conception, often embodying the crudest superstition, is reproduced in their conclusion, but now hallowed by the sacred name of 'science'.

The following are two examples of recent popular scientific approaches to the the question: 'What are humans?'

Thinking Machines?

Several powerful developments in science and technology during the past half-century have shaken up the way that humans think of themselves. The release of atomic energy, the development of molecular biology and the beginning of extraterrestrial travel are a few examples of scientific work which have suggested new standpoints from which our species can look at itself and at the planet on which it lives.

However, it is the all-pervasive electronic computer which has opened up some of the most startling questions. In the 1940s when they first appeared, these machines were commonly known as 'electronic brains'. Ever since then, the idea has been abroad that someone has manufactured machines which can think. On the one hand, the tasks given to computing machines were expected to encroach on many activities previously regarded as specifically those of humans. On the other, the machine was going to give us an insight into how our brains work.

Back in the 1930s, the papers of Alan Turing[5] on 'computable numbers' had theorised the possibility of mechanising intellectual operations. By 1950, when his even more famous paper appeared, computers actually existed. Now, he could pose the problem of whether they might be programmed to imitate a human so accurately that it would be impossible to tell them apart. (Turing wagered this would be technically feasible before the year 2000.)

The academic discipline called Artificial Intelligence (AI) soon got under way.[6] By the 1950s, research-workers were creating computer programmes which could, for example, recognise simple patterns, solve puzzles and play draughts and chess. In 1956, Newell and Simon announced:

> There are now in the world machines that think, that learn and that create. Moreover, their ability to do these things is going to increase rapidly until – in a visible future – the range of problems they can handle will be coextensive with the range to which the human mind has been applied. … Intuition, insight and learning are no longer the exclusive possession of humans: any large high-speed computer can be programmed to exhibit them also.[7]

Such euphoria was understandable. It had become clear that computers were not just machines for 'number-crunching', but systems for operating on symbols. Surely, as soon as the engineers had constructed machines of sufficient size and speed, any mental task would be programmable. The word 'information', a technical term used by telecommunications people, passed into everyday language. Computers were 'information processors', symbol manipulators. Were human brains anything else?

Struck by this analogy, schools of 'cognitive science' sprang up, combining psychology, neurophysiology and computer science. They have been encouraged by the development of so-called 'neural nets'. Many independent computational devices are connected together, and the strengths of the connections are altered in accordance with what the system does. Instead of setting out with a program of instructions, like the computers we all know, the 'connectionist' machine 'learns' from its own 'experience'.

The idea for this style of computer architecture comes directly from neuro-science. The hope of modelling a machine on the possible structure of the brain thus complemented the attempt to understand the brain as a kind of machine. I have no wish to underestimate the achievements of workers in this field, but it must be said that they have only changed the way that the problem posed by 'old-fashioned AI' is expressed.[8]

Buoyed up by unbounded optimism and massive research grants from military and industrial sources (in the US, almost entirely military), propagandists for AI kept making increasingly grandiose claims about what machines would do 'in the next decade'. Forty years on, some of them are still at it.

Violent criticism of these views appeared immediately, of course. One form that they often took was pretty futile. Where the AI supporters predicted wonders, their opponents drew a line which was alleged to separate things which machines could achieve from things which only humans could do. The ever-accelerating advance of the computer industry answered some of these challenges quite soon. Robots, equipped with the means to 'see' and 'hear', are now quite common in factories. So are machines which respond to humanly spoken words with their own version of language.

But as the machines grew more and more powerful and programming became increasingly sophisticated, doubts began to appear within the AI community itself.[9] What computers were now doing was amazing, but was it *thought*? Philosophers battled with AI practitioners over questions of intentionality, intelligence and emotion and the fight still goes on.

However, the opponents of the notion of machine intelligence usually start from a very similar outlook to that of their antagonists. For example, John Searle, well known for his philosophical attacks on the idea of machine intelligence, is sure that: 'Mental phenomena, all mental phenomena, whether conscious or unconscious, visual or auditory, pains, tickles, itches, thoughts, indeed, all of our mental life, are caused by processes going on in the brain.'[10] This is just what the AI people all believe too, and with a similar dogmatic certainty. Like them, Searle believes that thinking is an individual, private activity, as if it could be separated from language and culture. So he is quite happy with the idea that brains are machines. He only disagrees with the AI belief that computers are the same kind of machine.[11]

In the course of one of his writings on AI, Searle lets slip an interesting remark. He imagines an opponent asking him:

'Well, if programs are in no way constitutive of mental processes, why have so many people believed the converse? That at least needs some explanation.' I don't really know the answer to that one.[12]

It seems to me that *this* is the question which really matters. Why does Searle turn away from the confusion in people's minds about whether they are *themselves* automata? Is it not far more important than logical riddles about whether, and in what sense, these devices can be said to 'understand' what they are doing? AI itself is an expression of people's inability to control their own lives. The problem is to understand this pathological symptom of a world in which people are, indeed, made to think of *themselves* as purely mechanical.

The Sociobiology Affair

In 1971, E.O. Wilson's *The Insect Societies* was a best-seller among his fellow entomologists. However, when the same author published *Sociobiology: The New Synthesis* four years later, the stir it caused went far beyond this circle of insect buffs and, indeed, beyond the world of science.

For Wilson claimed to extend his explanation of the evolution of social behaviour from insects to the species *homo sapiens*. Its first chapter, 'The Morality of the Gene', declared that 'sociology and other social sciences, as well as the humanities, are the last branches of biology waiting to be included in the Modern Synthesis'.[13] And the final chapter was devoted exclusively to explaining how human social behaviour is 'genetically determined', just like that of ants and termites. Wilson lends his scientific prestige to statements like these: 'Among general social traits are aggressive dominance systems with males dominant over females'[14] and 'Man would rather believe than know.'[15]

The 600-page book was given a coffee-table format and considerable media hype. Reviews in scholarly journals and highbrow magazines were supplemented by features and interviews with Wilson in rather more mainstream, populist publications. (*House and Garden*: 'Getting Back to Nature – Our Hope for the Future'; *Readers Digest*: 'Why We Do What We Do'; *People Magazine*: 'A New Science with New Ideas on Why We Sometimes Behave Like Cavemen'.)

In 1978, Wilson produced yet another book, *On Human Nature*, which made even bigger claims:

The species lacks any goal external to its own biological nature.[16]

Innate censors and motivators exist in the brain that deeply and unconsciously affect our ethical premises; from these roots, morality evolved as an instinct. If that perception is correct, science may soon be in a position to investigate the very origin and meaning of human values, from which all ethical pronouncements and much of political practice flow. ...

Human emotional responses and the more general ethics based upon them have been programmed to a substantial degree by natural selection over thousands of generations.[17]

Human aggression, Wilson is quite sure, is 'innate', while

some of the most baffling religious practices in history might have an ancestry passing in a straight line back to the ancient carnivorous habits of humankind.[18]

The predisposition to religious belief is the most complex and powerful force in the human mind and in all probability an irradicable part of human nature.[19]

The sociobiological story is very simple, as its opponents have clearly explained. Being human is something inherited biologically. The way humans behave is determined by the genetic material with which they are born. The ways that we act, think and feel are 'programmed' in our genes. Behavioural patterns are the outcome of adaptation by natural selection. Choose pretty well any activity in which people engage, from sex to self-sacrifice, and it is child's play for a sociobiologist to find an ingenious 'scientific' explanation of how we got just this particular habit by selection of the appropriate genes. (Critical biologists like to refer derisively to such accounts as 'Just So Stories'.)

It's a pretty obvious trick. Anything humans are observed to do, any nasty habits they display, can be ascribed to a 'genetic predisposition'. If we are feeling a bit optimistic, or if we find something we don't want to fix in that way, we don't have to, since it can also be said to be caused by 'culture'. You just can't lose!

When Richard Dawkins, an expert in animal behaviour, published his celebrated *The Selfish Gene* in 1976, he went even further than Wilson: 'We are survival machines – robot vehicles blindly programmed to preserve the selfish molecules known as genes.'[20]

Over the past decade or so sociobiology has grown into a major academic industry. Some of the more absurd statements of over-enthusiastic practitioners have been toned down, but by no means all. Sometimes its operatives speak of sociobiology itself as 'a science', while on other occasions they more modestly call it 'a scientific theory'.

'Behaviour' is inseparable from thought and feeling, so the development of evolutionary psychology might have been predicted. On the other hand, the application of sociobiology to economics is perhaps more surprising.[21] In 1975, the readers of *Business Week*, were delighted to learn, under the headline 'The Genetic Defense of the Free Market', that 'competitive self-interest, the bioeconomists say, has its origins in the human gene pool'.

The manner in which Wilson and his friends invoke 'science' is interesting. The very word is used as if it must necessarily silence all dissent, very like the use of biblical quotations in former times. But we should not be intimidated: all their claims ought be examined with care. For example, just what are these 'genes' which they tell us are the determining subject in all our lives? They are supposed to pull the strings which make us all jump, but they are never defined except in the vaguest terms. Reading the arrogant statements of the sociobiologists, it is sometimes difficult to remember that they are actually unable to point to a particular bit of genetic material which can be said to cause a single piece of animal or plant behaviour – let alone human behaviour.

The way that some scientists now think of human beings is strikingly illustrated by the mountains of dollars being lavished on the Human Genome Project, the plan to 'map' human DNA. In order to bolster their demands for this cash – the rest of biological research in the US is under severe threat, as the Project hoovers up all the available funds – its supporters throw around unlimited claims for what they can achieve.

Here, for instance, is Walter Gilbert, Harvard Professor of Molecular Biology:

> Three billion bases of sequence can be put on a single compact disk, and one will be able to pull a CD out of one's pocket and say, 'Here is a human being; it's me!' ... To recognise that we are determined, in a certain sense, by a finite collection of information that is knowable will change our view of ourselves.[22]

Sociobiologists talk about the modern version of the theory of evolution as if it were identical with biological science and they can take its approach for granted when 'applying' it to *homo sapiens*. In fact, the whole approach is challenged by some of the leading figures in contemporary biology.[23]

Charles Darwin, from whom all modern biologists claim (intellectual) descent, had no concept of genetics, of course. The characteristics of an organism were passed down to its offspring, with some changes, but Darwin did not claim to know any special mechanism for this process. Although he had been sent a copy of Mendel's work on inheritance, he never read it. Genetics became linked with evolution only after considerable controversy. Julian Huxley's book, *Evolution: The Modern Synthesis*, combining Darwin's natural selection with Mendel's genetics, came out only in 1942. (Wilson's 1975 book was named in honour of Huxley's.)

When, in 1953, Crick and Watson announced their discovery of the 'genetic code' in the structure of DNA, Mendel's gene was thenceforward considered as a bit of DNA, which somehow 'controlled' the development of the organism, whether plant, ant, elephant or human. Weissmann's doctrine of the 'continuity of the germ-plasm' was translated into Crick's 'Central Dogma': information flows *from* DNA, not *into* it.

What happened to the theory of evolution seems to have been something like this. In the last century, biologists sought in Darwin's idea of natural selection a way of imitating the success of the rival science, physics. The secret, they came to believe, was to reduce the working of the complexities with which they were faced to the actions of simpler entities.

They could not begin with the world as a whole (with all its interconnections) as the unity whose development was to be understood. Instead, they wanted to start with the simplest possible biological component, and then build up from there. A single instance of the chosen unit is contrasted with everything else, called its 'environment'. Natural selection is then supposed to be about the adaptation of the organism to its environment. But, however difficult it makes our task, we cannot brush aside the fact that this 'environment' itself contains other evolving, active units. Each of these is itself an organic assembly of evolving sub-units.

So even before the evolution of humankind comes into the story, the ground on which sociobiology stands is shaky. Once humanity enters into the picture, the problems of evolutionary theory are multiplied a thousandfold. Ever since Darwin, biology has always had as its target the explanation of the origin and function of human society, the most intricate of totalities. But biology is itself a *part* of human society. Darwin tells us that the idea of natural selection began to form in his mind after his reading of Malthus's *Essay on Population*.

Of course, the process of selective inheritance must play an important part in the development of species of organism, and that must include humans. But that does not mean that evolution is a matter of selective inheritance *alone*, separate from the forms of activity of the individual organism, the rest of its species and the ecological system in which they live.

Sociobiology evoked violent opposition among prominent US radical biologists and philosophers.[24] Many of them charged Wilson and his co-thinkers with giving support to racism and sexism. Some of these critics considered themselves 'Marxists' and 'dialectical materialists', and accused sociobiology of being part of the ideological defence of inequality.[25]

But, as in the case of AI – the two are often closely associated – I do not think these critics got to the heart of the matter. Beyond generalities about the connection of Wilson's ideas to 'the maintenance of the existing social order', they did not seem to ask themselves why this particular argument arose just when it did. It must go deeper than that. The way we look at ourselves must have something to do with the way people treat each other, including the way they treat themselves. The attempt to explain human life in purely biological terms is founded on a view of the human species as a whole which arises from their inhuman way of life.

Theories about Humans

Medical science is among the oldest branches of knowledge. Its successes in modern times are justly celebrated. But, as is well known, its outlook assumes that the human body is a collection of interrelated parts. Each specialisation treats a different bit of what is regarded as a very complex machine. No-one is concerned with the human as a whole. Even the manner of the typical medical practitioner expresses this attitude, which is bound up with the attempt to separate the expert from the 'patient', who, however, just happens to be a fellow human.

These difficulties of natural science show themselves again in the confusions of 'green' politics. The development of ecology as a scientific study tries to look at entire systems of plant and animal life and the balance between them. How, then, is the species *homo sapiens* to be seen in such a context? 'Greens' often appear to want to down-grade the human with respect to the rest of the natural world. Some of them talk as though we had no business to be here at all.

But it is in the alleged 'social sciences' that the approach I am criticising shows its problematic character most blatantly. Economics, sociology, anthropology and so on display what the palaeontologist Stephen J. Gould calls 'physics envy': the desire of those trying to study society 'scientifically' to emulate their natural-scientific colleagues. They struggle for quantification and mathematisation. They yearn for rigorous definitions and axioms. They build 'models' of humanity and strain every muscle in the attempt to validate them statistically. And in the background of such theoretical work lurks the shadow of its application to 'social engineering'.

Econometrics is a good example of such an approach. It ignores everything about economic life, except the levels at given times of a finite number of variable quantities – GNP, money-supply, unemployment, price levels and so on. Then it sets up an algebraic system of relationships and, using economic data, tries to make statistical estimates of the 'parameters' of the chosen model. The key feature of such econometric models is the total absence of anything resembling a human being, anything which feels, suffers, enjoys or thinks, or indeed anything other than pure quantity.

The more rigorous the methods of a 'social science', the less it seems to have to do with humanity, and the more easily what is essentially human escapes capture. Each social science uses a different model of humanity, and none of them takes any notice of the ones employed by the rest. None of them sees the whole picture. As we have seen, a model must begin by defining those aspects of its subject-matter which it is trying to relate. Each definition begs all the questions I want to ask, especially about how the world might be made to differ fundamentally from its present state.

There are some trends in recent scientific development which make similar objections to these. Particularly in the last twenty years, several fields have opened up which challenge the view of the world as a collection of bits and pieces, and quite deliberately study structure, complexity, wholeness. Many thinkers have emphasised the differences between the study of nature and that of humanity. This work is indeed of great importance and underlines some of the deficiencies I have been talking about. However, the question it never seems to examine is *why*? *Why* does 'orthodoxy' take the positions criticised?

As I said earlier, if someone comes up with what they claim is an explanation of human life, they really ought to show how their explanation explains *itself*. Where in this picture of the world can you find their own thoughts and feelings which drove them to ask these questions and struggle to find these particular answers? Science is itself a human activity, albeit one in which only a tiny minority of people engage. But if its notion of the human is false, there is no way it can understand itself.

The methods I have been discussing explicitly renounce the chance to look at themselves. The picture of humanity drawn by such methods has necessarily to be a view from the outside. That is why it depicts a collection of individual beings, separated from each other, and each fragmented into many uncoordinated pieces. Their lives conform to fixed, predefined modes of being, which, individually and collectively, they are powerless to change.

But isn't there something strangely familiar about this picture? Indeed there is. It is just like the *inhuman* way we humans actually live. And this is the heart of our difficulty. Forms of knowledge are engendered by the very way that we live, which prevent us from grasping the truth about ourselves and our way of life.

The problems we face at the end of the millennium are bound up with our inability to understand ourselves and the relations between us. Natural science studies all kinds of objects, but it cannot see the one nearest home – ourselves. It seeks the truth only by placing a barrier between itself and the object. Why does science behave like this? Do the causes lie inside science itself, or outside, in the very world it cannot see? What is there about the way that we live which induces this strange myopia about the relation between science and humanity?

Surely, it is significant that humans have the very possibility of asking the question, what is it to be human? Ants or pigs or dandelions neither know nor care about who *they* are, so why should we? And this problem raises another: if we are clever enough to pose such riddles – and some people have been doing so for thousands of years – why have we been so slow at finding answers? So any answer to the question, 'what is it to be human?', must deal some others: How is it that we, unlike any other kind of object, can ask such a question? How has the answer been hidden from us for so long, and why do most people go right through their lives *without* asking it? How must we think and how must we act to bring an answer to light?

And that brings us back to Marx.

Marx and Method

Marx worked to produce a *science of liberation*, the implications of which I am trying to establish. 'Marxism', making a great noise about 'the Marxist method', always separated the activity called science from the process through which humanity emancipated itself. If it got round to discussing communist society at all, it was always prefaced by remarks about how Marx avoided the futility of utopianism. The scientific method attributed to Marx was then only a variant of the method of bourgeois science. The difference was supposed to be confined to the 'application' of Marx's results to political struggle.

The Eleventh Thesis on Feuerbach is famous (and is inscribed on Marx's tomb): 'Philosophers have hitherto interpreted the world in different ways: the point, however, is to change it.'

This has often been assumed by the 'Marxist' tradition to mean: theorise a bit, and then get on with the real job of 'making a revolution'. This misses the whole point. Marx is not talking about either 'interpreting' or 'changing the world' in some general sense. He is concerned with the specific problem of how to liberate humanity from its inhuman way of life. He focussed on the particular question: what is it to be human? It could not be just a matter of 'interpretation', important as that might be. It could only be tackled in terms of a *task*: what must we *do* to live humanly?

Throughout history, great thinkers, whose works remain vital for our own time, have striven to illuminate what they saw as the most important issues of human life. Indeed, this was the best that they could do, given the social conditions under which they worked. (Marx's admiration for Aristotle, and his attitude to the limitation of Aristotle's understanding by the institution of slavery, is a good example.[26]) But the conditions of modern society make it both possible and necessary to tackle questions which go *beyond the bounds of philosophical thinking*. That is the root opposition between Marx's science and all forms of utopia.

When Marx analysed the inhuman forms assumed by human life, he did not follow the course of established, 'normal' science. He did not begin by defining his object, then, keeping himself totally separated from his well-defined object, try to express the logical consequences of this definition. On the contrary, including himself in the picture, he showed that humanity was potentially free to define itself. He had to trace the path through which humanity would liberate itself from the forms which enclosed it and falsified its self-image. The problem was to grasp how humanity can achieve consciousness *of itself*.

In Volume 3 of *Capital* is an often-quoted statement: '[A]ll science would be superfluous if the form of appearance of things directly coincided with their essence.'[27] I used to be delighted with this boost for theoretical thinking. But this led me to ignore other questions which hovered in the background. *Why* are the appearance and essence of social forms separated? *Why* is science required to bridge the gap? Where did it plant its feet when it did this job? How can its intellectual activity alter anything in practice?

Marx not only wants to know what gives science the power to penetrate surface appearance. He is even more interested in the question: *why is it such hard work*? Even Hegel, Adam Smith and Ricardo were incapable of asking such questions. To pose such problems, we must imagine another sort of world, where the relations between human beings are transparent to them, because these relations are consciously made by them.

I am not talking about the way that humans, rational beings, go about their rational lives. I am discussing life under the monstrous power of capital. What reigns in this world, masquerading as Reason, persuading us that it is built into the very fabric of reality, is actually *in*humanity, *madness*. Here, nothing appears as it really is.

Is this God's will? Both Hegel and Adam Smith knew that it is not. It is all *our* doing. Like the man fatally hooked on heroin, *we* are doing it – and it's killing us. But now I am not talking philosophy! Just as the addict cannot *reason* his way out of his predicament, these problems cannot be answered in thought alone, but only in conscious, purposive activity, in life, in 'revolutionising practice', activity which can render it human.

Karl Marx and Some Theories

Theory and Political Economy

Marx's problem was this: what must we *do* if we are to become *self-conscious* and *self-creative*, that is, truly human? I have tried to show that this problem cannot be answered in a 'theory', because that would imply assuming a defined limit for the answer sought. While 'Marxism' certainly embodied several theories, Karl Marx was not in that business at all.

Let us look yet again at Marx's chief work, *Capital*. Its title-page tells us that it is *a Critique of Political Economy*, and that its first volume is about *The Production-Process of Capital*, that is, how the inhuman relation, capital, produces and reproduces itself. But we should not be misled by those mistranslations of this work into English – including the one that Engels authorised, I'm afraid – which declare themselves to be about the '*Critical Analysis of Capitalist Production*'. That is *not* what Marx wrote. Engels mistitled the second and third volumes, too.

Marx (who, we must not forget, was a communist), was investigating how the set of exploitative, oppressive relations which dominated the working class, and consequently the whole of human life, came to seem perfectly 'natural', an expression of 'human nature'. Forms of thought which enshrined this misconception played an essential part in the way that society operated: 'How could people live without money, wages, employers?', 'If I did not have a slave-owner, who would feed me?' Such questions seem to be purely rhetorical.

Capital was Marx's name for the core of the social relations which prevail in modern society. It was a vast, impersonal power, which forced us all continually to produce and reproduce it. When this was clearly understood, the struggle of the working class against the power of capital could be seen for what it really was: the struggle for a human life, by people treated inhumanly, used as if they were things or machines.

Now, was this a 'theory'? I believe it was nothing of the kind. As we have seen, the essential nature of a theory is that it stops us from criticising the 'something' we are trying to theorise. Once we have put our object inside its fence, drawn up our category-list and switched on our method, we are stuck with them. To say that the object ought to be different, or ought not to *be* at all, is not allowed by the rules of the theory-game. Anyone expressing sentiments like these will instantly get a red card and will be sent off for being untheoretical or *ethical*. Why? Because these rules are themselves a reflection of the set-up we are trying to theorise.

But that was the whole point of Marx's revolutionary enterprise. I think that the method Marx uses *is* ethical in character. I mean that it embodies his conception of what human beings are, how they could live humanly and how they actually live inhumanly in bourgeois society. He criticises the method of political economy because he knows that the categories it uses arise from the inhuman nature of society itself. He possesses a criterion with which to condemn the existing set-up and builds it into his investigation.

In *Capital* he shows that the exchange of objects for money presents the relations between people in a 'crazy [*verrückte*] form', adding:

> The categories of bourgeois economics consist precisely of forms of this kind. They are forms of thought which are socially valid, and therefore objective, for the relations of production belonging to this historically determined mode of social production.[28]

Thus the 'better' the theory, the more clearly it portrays capital as if it were logical, the more misleading it is, because the capitalist mode of production is itself a lie, a form of human life which denies humanity.

Marx's enterprise was scientific, a search for systematic, universal knowledge. But what does he want to do with this knowledge? If he had been in the theory business, he would have been aiming at an 'explanatory framework', one which 'explained' the existing economic system better than any alternative interpretation. But that was not what he was trying to do at all.

Capital contains not one, but two sets of terms. One set is taken straight from the category-list of the scientific political economy of Adam Smith and David Ricardo. These terms – for example, 'value', 'profit' and 'wages' – which describe the way that capital operates, but mask its inhuman nature, are developed in a way which tears off this mask. By criticising them, Marx is opening the road for the 'criticism-by-revolution' of the world they theorise.

But there is also a second set of terms, invented specially by Marx. Terms like 'abstract labour', 'surplus value' and 'rate of exploitation' are used to reveal the *real* story, which the other categories serve to mystify: the imprisonment of human life within the inhuman shell of the bourgeois mode of production. To get hold of terms like this, Marx had to check and critically assess the entire range of theoretical equipment of the political economists.

When Marx derives a ratio between two quantities and calls it 'the rate of exploitation', he is deliberately *not* being 'theoretical'. When he describes the devastating effect of the division of labour on the worker, the sufferings of women and children during the industrial revolution, struggles over the length of the working day, the fate of peasants cleared from the land on which they lived, or the revival of slavery in a capitalist form in the New World, he is quite clearly talking about the *inhumanity* of capital and of the economists who apologise for it.

Marx sees that the division of capital into two parts, *fixed* and *circulating*, arises from the way that capital appears to the capitalists and their theoretical spokesmen. But this, he shows, falsifies the nature of capital. Instead, Marx introduces the division between *constant* and *variable* capital. The first covers raw material, machinery, etc., while the second takes the form of the wages bill. This is how Marx spotlights the separation of the instruments of production from the producers by the capitalist form of private property, and the ability of capital to extract a surplus from the labour of the wage worker. Thus he brings out the way that human creativity is dehumanised in modern society.

> The relation of exchange between capitalist and worker becomes a mere semblance, belonging only to the process of circulation, it becomes a mere form, which is alien to the content of the transaction itself, and merely mystifies it. The constant sale and purchase of labour-power is the form; the content is the constant appropriation by the capitalist, without equivalent, of a portion of the labour of

others, which has already been objectified, and his repeated exchange of this labour for a greater quantity of the living labour of others. ... The separation of property from labour thus becomes the necessary consequence of a law that apparently originated in their identity.[29]

The 'Marxist' notion that Marx had developed a new kind of political economy, a set of 'economic doctrines', including a 'theory of value', got it all wrong. Marx began with all the assumptions of the great classical political economists and showed how they concealed a reality which was their direct contrary. A 'theory of value', like that of Ricardo, as a theory, is obliged to maintain the story that the relations of bourgeois society are the expression of 'human nature', that the exchange of equivalents is necessary for human life and human freedom.

That was why Marx valued the work of these writers so highly. It was objective science, and that was why he spent so much effort on the long manuscript known as *Theories of Surplus Value*. This was devoted to the development of bourgeois economics, from 'classical', scientific political economy, to the later economists whom he described as 'vulgar', and for whom he had the most profound contempt. In other words, it was a careful study and criticism of *other people's* theories.

Science, philosophy and utopia each has a dual relation to the estranged world. At their best, they express the need to answer questions about the opposition of existing society to what it might be. But methodologically they take this same opposition as fixed and immutable. In their different ways, each of them views the world through its own set of categories, which are accepted without comment. To the scientist, the categories of his or her own speciality are invisible.

Marx's simultaneous critique of the categories of political economy, of utopian socialism and of Hegel does not aim to replace them with an improved set. He grasps them as expressions of the way that humanity is concealed within inhumanity. By tracing their logical interconnections, he finds the way to break their stranglehold on our consciousness and on our lives.

'Obviously the Correct Scientific Method'

I have not often used the word 'dialectic' in this discussion. The story about 'dialectical materialism' is so widely accepted that it comes as a shock to discover that this word 'dialectic' crops up very seldom in Marx's works. It does appear a few times in *Grundrisse*, but it is not used consistently. So, for thirty years, in public, Marx used it exclusively to mean *Hegel's* dialectic.

Only in 1873, in the 'Afterword' to the second edition of *Capital*, does he 'avow' himself 'a pupil of that mighty thinker' and refer to 'my dialectical method'. Just look at this reference:

My dialectical method is, in its foundation, not only different from the Hegelian, but its direct opposite. For Hegel, the thought-process, which he even transforms into an independent subject, under the name of 'the Idea', is the creator of the actual, and the actual is only the external appearance of the Idea. With me, the reverse is true: the ideal is nothing more than the real movement, overturned and translated in the human head.[30]

(I quote this famous paragraph in a slightly altered translation. The substitution of 'the real movement' for 'the material' is justified by the French translation which Marx made at about the same time: *'Materielle'* there appears as *'le mouvement réal'*.)

Befuddled by the 'dialectical materialist' myth, generations of Marxists, including Marx's mis-translators, have read this as a recommendation to disconnect Hegel's excellent dialectical method from his unfortunate idealist theory of knowledge and then hitch it up to a healthy materialist outlook. In this way, the entire *human* meaning of Marx's insight was buried, while at the same time we were cut off from a true understanding of Hegel's achievement. (I won't go into it here, but I contend, first, that it is misleading to call Hegel an idealist, and, second, that neither he nor Marx had a 'theory of knowledge'. See the Appendix to this chapter.)

Marx's work did not aim at setting up a scientific 'model' of the world, nor an explanation of 'how it worked', nor an 'interpretation' of it. His object was something rather different from pigs or God or atoms: *humanity itself*. With *this* as his object, he could not leave himself outside.

When Marx was examining the theories of the political economists, he was also concerned with the problem of the nature of science. Section 3 of his 1857 Introduction to *Grundrisse*,[31] the section entitled 'The Method of Political Economy', examined it in some detail. So let us spend some time looking at this widely discussed – and widely misunderstood – text.

Almost universally (I know of only one exception, the book by Hiroshi Uchida,[32] although there may be others), it is taken to be a description of *Marx's own* method, which somehow managed to be the same as both Ricardo's and Hegel's. The passage is usually presented as if it were a kind of advertisement, something like this:

A satisfied customer, Dr Marx, writes: 'Just watch thought advance from the Simple to the mental concrete: this is definitely *the* way to discover the truth.'

This would be an odd way to introduce a book devoted to the *critique* of political economy, founded on the *critique* of Hegel's dialectic. Before jumping to 'Marxist' conclusions, it is a good idea to look at what Marx actually wrote, which necessitates a careful check on English translations.[33]

Marx thought the political economists had two main ways of getting started with their theory construction. First of all, he refers to the seventeeth-century political economists – he has in mind, particularly, William Petty – and their habit of beginning with what seemed to be 'the real and concrete', for example, population, nation, state. 'It seems to be right to begin with the real and concrete, the actual conditions.'[34]

But does that mean *he* accepts this approach? Of course not. This is how the Introduction to *Grundrisse* proceeds:

> However, under closer scrutiny, this shows itself to be false ... a chaotic conception of the whole ... through closer determination I would, gradually, come to simpler notions; from the imagined concrete to ever thinner abstractions, until I reached the simplest determination. ...
>
> The [political] economists of the 17th century ... always end up with finding out, through analysis, some determining, abstract, general relations, like division of labour, money, value, etc.

Now he turns to their eighteenth-century successors, thinking of Adam Smith especially, of course. They tried going the other way. Starting with the simple, and progressively getting more complex, they made a return journey, 'until, finally, I reached [my starting-point], this time, however, not as a chaotic representation of a whole, but as a rich totality of many determinations and relations'. Along this second path, 'the abstract determinations lead to the reproduction of the concrete by way of thinking'. This may look more scientific, but it all depends on what you mean by science. Like other 'Marxists', I used to be quite sure that Marx approved of this second path and built himself a theory by means of it. Now I no longer believe this.

Marx's next sentence, read with all the fixed prejudices of 'Marxism', has led to enormous confusion: 'The latter is obviously the correct scientific method.' At least, that is what it *seems* to say. Since these eight words provide the *only* foundation for the usual reading of this entire text, we had better examine the fine print: '*Das leztre ist offenbar die wis-*

senschaftlich richtige Methode.' In fact, '*offenbar*', as well as 'obviously', means 'evidently', 'manifestly' or even 'seemingly'. So, Marx is saying *this* way *also* seems right.

He goes on to give us some reasons why we might think so – and then why he does not:

> The concrete is concrete because it is the gathering together [*Zusammenfassung*] of many determinations, that is unity of the manifold. In thinking, therefore, it appears as a process of gathering together, as a result, not as a starting point, although it is the real starting point, and therefore also the starting point of perception [*Anschauung*] and representation [*Vorstellung*].

So we have two opposite ways of going about our investigation. 'The first procedure evaporates the full visualisation into abstract determination; along the second, the abstract determinations lead to the reproduction of the concrete by way of thinking.' I am convinced that Marx does not see why he should choose *either* of these approaches. Otherwise, the entire character of Section 3 – 'but', '*ça dépend*', 'still', 'on the other hand' – makes no sense. Rather, he is saying that, while the second approach might be the right way to theorise, *why theorise at all?*

Without any explanation, the next passage takes us straight to Hegel. Fourteen years earlier, Marx had made a careful critique of Hegel's philosophy of the state, and another of 'Hegel's Dialectic and Philosophy as a Whole'. In the latter manuscript, he declares that 'Hegel's standpoint is that of modern political economy.' Now, he returns to that idea, combining his critique of Hegel with his critique of Ricardo and Smith.[35]

Talk about 'Marx the materialist' versus 'Hegel the idealist' has obscured what Marx was doing. He found in Hegel's system, philosophy at its highest point, the essence of what he was criticising in the great classical political economists. Speaking on behalf of the entire philosophical tradition, Hegel attempts the feat of scaling 'the Absolute', 'the Unconditioned'. The entire human world, with all its contradictions – appearance and essence, good and evil, triumph and failure – has to be hauled inside the logical-historical movement he called dialectic. Then the dialectical door is bolted behind it. Now, the Absolute Method can provide itself with its own raw material, its own instruments of production and its own foundations.

Here, in this highly abstract form, in Hegel's Absolute, Marx finds the secret of political economy, of the exploitative, oppressive, self-sustaining character of bourgeois society, of the appearance that it is 'natural' and of the path to its revolutionary transcendence. This is how the Introduction brings Hegel into the story:

> Hegel, therefore, fell into the illusion of taking the real as a result of gathering itself together [*Zusammenfassung*], delving into itself, and moving out on its own; whereas the method of ascending from the abstract to the concrete is only the way for thinking to appropriate the concrete, to reproduce it as a mental [*geistige* = spiritual] concrete ... For consciousness, therefore – and this is how philosophical consciousness is determined – for whom a thinking that grasps notions [*begreifende Denken*] as the real human being and only the world notionally grasped [*begriffne*] as such as the real – the movement of the categories appears, therefore, to be the real act of production ...

Precisely as in 1844, Marx is associating Hegel's logic with the method of political economy and criticising both of them. The kind of thinking which 'reproduces the concrete as a spiritual concrete' is exactly what Marx was to call '*fetishism*'. This is a false, abstract way of thinking, not because it does not correspond accurately to the actual way in which people live, think and feel today, but because it *does* correspond to them. It is the object, this particular way of life, which is false and abstract. The fetishised thinking which arises from it 'fits' it and makes it appear 'natural'.

The whole, as it appears in the head as a thought-whole [*Gedankenganzes*] is a product of the thinking head, which appropriates the world in the only manner possible for it, a manner which differs fom the artistic-, religious-, practical-spiritual [*geistigen*] assimilation of this world. As before, the real subject remains in its independence outside the head; that is, so long as the head behaves only speculatively, only theoretically.

Marx has got to the heart of the problem. Capital is the active subject in bourgeois society which dominates and destroys human life. How does it reproduce itself as a social relation in such a way that it appears to all who live inside its impersonal, inhuman and totally crazy world to be perfectly natural and perfectly rational? Hegel's logical scheme, dialectic, gives us the clue to the answer. By tucking its actual assumption – the existence of bourgeois society – inside its beginning, it performs its dialectical magic trick. 'Look', it cries, 'no presuppositions!' As Marx puts it: 'Capital is the economic power that dominates everything in bourgeois society. It must form both point of departure and the conclusion.'[36]

Thus we see that Hegel's dialectical logic is essential for Marx's critique of political economy because both Hegel and political economy base themselves on the same conception of what humanity *is*. That is why Marx's critique of that logic – and thus of the logic of capital – is inseparable from his communism. To believe, as Hegel does, that the real human being is 'the comprehending mind', is equivalent to restricting 'the real world' to 'the comprehended world'. This means banning those questions which go beyond pre-set bounds of what is askable: world history, as it is known, has been fixed as the only one possible.

What characterises both Adam Smith and Hegel is precisely this completion of the circle of categories. It locks us all – bourgeois and proletarians – into the prison ruled over by capital. Some prisoners might have considerable privileges, while others are condemned to hard labour or even to death. But we are each forced into the miserable prison uniform of the economic category we happen to personify. Under the iron control of the invisible hand, or of the Idea, the relations between subject and object, living and dead, active and passive have been reversed.

The characteristics of humanity which were most important to Marx were its powers of *creativity* and *self-creativity*. In the course of what he called 'the social production of their life', humans *defined themselves* in their practice. In the conditions of class division, exploitation, oppression and struggle, mental and physical activities are rigidly separated. As a result, we are unconscious of the collective process of self-creation in which we are engaged. We create ourselves with our eyes shut. Not surprisingly, we make a complete mess of it. The 'theoretical method' accurately reflects the characteristics of this 'estranged' way of life. In political economy, 'the categories express forms of being, determinations of existence and sometimes only individual aspects – of this particular society'.[37] That is how Marx explored simultaneously the falsity of three things: these categories, the method which employs them and the society they expressed.

Political Economy and Religion

Throughout his writings, Marx often connected the ideas of money, logic and religion, and his attitude to religion might help to illustrate his critical method. Marx did not believe that religion was just a con-trick, a false story spread by priests to maintain class rule. (It was often like that, but not always, and never *only* so.)

Religion sprang from the real suffering of real people. As the famous passage in the *Introduction to the Critique of Hegel's Philosophy of Law* (1844) explains: 'Man makes religion, religion does not make man.' Religion is *an inverted world-consciousness*, produced by society and state,

> because they are an *inverted world*. Religion is the general theory of that world, its encyclopaedic compendium, its logic in a popular form, its spiritualistic *point d'honneur*, its enthusiasm, its moral sanction, its solemn complement, its universal source of consolation and justification. ... *Religious* distress is at the same time the *expression* of real distress and also the *protest* against real distress. Religion is the sigh of the oppressed creature, the heart of a heartless world, just as it is the spirit of spiritless conditions. It is the *opium* of the people. To abolish religion as the *illusory* happiness of the people is to demand their *real* happiness. The demand to give up illusions is the *demand to give up a state of affairs which needs illusions*.[38]

Note the *theoretical* nature of religious illusion. Like a 'theory', religious illusion objectively reflects the *real* world, precisely because it is a world where people cannot live without illusions.

I think that Marx's relation to political economy is as follows. Because the world of money is upside-down, inverted forms of thought are needed to give it theoretical expression with objective validity. The critique of political economy and of its crazy forms of thought therefore takes us to the heart of the struggle to transcend this craziness.

In *Capital*, Marx explains that: 'The religious reflections of the real world can ... vanish only when the practical relations of everyday life between man and man, and man and nature, generally present themselves to him in a transparent and rational form.'[39] In a similar way, the disappearance of political economy is bound up with the disappearance of the crazy forms of life of which it is a theoretical expression. Just as religion is not simply a 'mistake', to be rectified by logical argument, so political economy is not a set of 'mistakes'. Indeed, the great achievement of Smith and Ricardo, Marx believed, was to give objective expression to a 'mistaken' reality.

A Theory of History?

'Marxism' believed itself to be a 'historical materialism', a materialist conception of history, or a 'theory of history'. I don't think this describes Marx's view at all. Anyone who thinks it does should read the letter Marx wrote to the Russian journal *Otechestvenniye Zapiski*. Marx derides those who attribute to him 'a general historico-philosophical theory, the supreme virtue of which consists in its being superhistorical'.[40] He illustrates his point with a reference to the fate of the peasantry in ancient Rome, and contrasts this with developments in Western Europe: 'Thus events strikingly analogous but taking place in different historical surroundings led to totally different results.'[41] Marx wrote the letter to contradict those 'Marxists' who saw developments in Russia as inevitably following a path directly parallel with that described in *Capital*.

For Marx, history was the process in which humans engaged in 'the social production of their life'. In this process of becoming human, they developed means and powers of production. But the forms of social relations within which this took place *denied* their humanity, their capacity for free self-creation. These social relations of production were 'independent of their will', imposed on them from the past, unfree.[42]

Their consciousness of these relations 'corresponded to' legal, political, religious and philosophic forms which made up a 'superstructure', built on top of this set of relations. So their social consciousness was 'determined' by the false, inhuman way that they lived and related to each other. Law, politics, religion and so on were the *illusory* ways in which we vainly attempted to resolve the conflict between humanity and inhumanity, and between individuals and the collective movement. This conflict was expressed in social revolution, as human potential developed and collided with inhuman forms of society, giving rise to new forms in which they can resume their development.

Note that the Preface to the *Critique of Political Economy* does not say anything about the socialist revolution, which has to be a conscious struggle for the emancipation of humanity from its last inhuman, 'antagonistic' form. It notes only that the productive forces which have developed within this form now provide 'the material conditions for a solution of this antagonism'.[43]

Is it right to call this a *theory*? I believe it is not. It is neither an *explanation* of history nor an *interpretation*, but an outline of the way humanity will break free of domination by all such explanations and interpretations. Certainly, it involved Marx in a systematic study of as much history and as many theories of history as he could manage, just as he had to study the entire history of political-economic theory and many other fields. But this study begins and ends with 'the social production of our life'. It was and is a study of humanity, undertaken by a human being, not by a professor who pretends to stand outside or above his subject-matter, while actually being just an unthinking part of it.

Theory and the State

Did Marx have a theory of the state? I do not believe so. We know that he considered the state to be 'the illusory community',[44] and that ought to be thought about. 'Marxism' talked a lot about the state as 'an instrument of violent class oppression'. As with the cruder descriptions of religion, this is true but misses Marx's point.

The state is a power standing outside and above society, but springing from its inhuman form. It tries to resolve the contradictions of society but cannot succeed. Its pretence to represent society as a whole is false. To believe that a theory of the state is possible is to believe that it is a kind of machine, a regulating mechanism, working outside human consciousness and desire. Of course, if this were true, there would be no way to overthrow it or to think about overthrowing it.

That is why Marx never spoke of a 'workers' state' through which the proletariat would in some sense 'hold power' in the transition to socialism. And in his writings on the Paris Commune of 1871, he was careful not to describe the Commune as a state. Rather, it was 'a working-class form of government'.

Conclusion

In order to evaluate the 'Marxist' tradition, we must try to read what Marx actually wrote, not what we imagine he wrote, or what we think he *ought* to have written. So long as we are encumbered with the 'Marxist' prejudice that he was engaged in constructing a 'theory', or if we think he had a 'method' operating outside his conception of communism, this is not possible. If we listen carefully to what he is saying everything becomes much simpler.

Theory is a form of thinking which reflects that inhuman shell in which our lives are covered, taking it for granted that humanity can never escape. Marx's struggle for communist revolution is centred on revealing this imprisonment, allowing us to regard it from a human standpoint and to find a way out. Instead of 'seeking science in his mind' and presenting a theory, Marx wanted to *free* our consciousness from these shackles. It is *that* insight which must be recaptured if communism is to be regenerated.

The way we live and the way we think about it are parts of the same problem. When humans live inhumanly, their self-conscious, social being is constricted and distorted inside a form in which their lives are atomised and their collective self-creation hidden. Marx's ideas are based on the struggle of the proletariat to realise its humanity. This is the force which strives against capital from the inside, working to break out of its alienated form of life. To give this fight scientific expression, to 'become its mouthpiece', Marx studied human life from 'the standpoint of human society, of socialised humanity'. His object was revealed by him as the outcome of social activity, so that it could be remade consciously.

Marx grasped the possibility of concepts which united science as a subjective activity and its object. They were separated by theory, the kind of abstraction which governed the lives of human beings living inside inhuman, estranged forms. Marx's science was concrete, live knowledge which we can use humanly. Of these two forms of knowledge, one expressed our enslavement, the other the road to our liberation.

Marx did not first construct a theory, which could later be applied to social problems if so desired. His science was *human* science, basing itself on humanity as a collectively self-constituting set of universal individuals. Such a science, and only such a science, could show humanity the way to break out of its inhuman shell.

Appendix:
Science and Humanity – Hegel, Marx and Dialectic*

It was in the 1890s, when Karl Marx had been safely dead for a decade, that Kautsky and Plekhanov invented 'Marxism'. This total falsification of Marx's work incorporated a story about a couple of 'Young Hegelians', who extracted the 'dialectical method' from Hegel's system, and transplanted it into a materialist world-view. Then – so ran the tale – they could 'apply' materialism to history. The inventors of 'Marxism' gave their mythical beast the name 'dialectical materialism'.

This fable about Marx was bound up with with another one – equally false – about Hegel. It was a stirring philosophical yarn about an 'Idealist', who believed that the world was made of mind-stuff, of which ordinary matter was no more than a shadow. This ghost-world jerked forward in a contradictory, automated dance called 'dialectic'. Spirit, exuding a strong religious odour, pulled the strings which kept History moving, individual humans being mere puppets, and not very life-like ones either. The state, which took charge of the workings of society, was supposedly modelled by Hegel on the authoritarian Prussian state.

* Reprinted from *Common Sense*, 15, April 1994.

Many people nowadays know that this is a caricature of the real Hegel. In this respect, he is luckier than Marx, who is still either attacked or praised as if he were indeed the figure depicted by 'Marxism'. (Although the 'Marxists' swallowed the Hegel legend whole, it would be unfair to blame them for it, since it was concocted by the 'Hegelians'.)

In order to contribute to the work of correcting these stereotypes, I want to focus on the meaning each of these two thinkers gives to the word 'science'. I argue that to think Marx and Hegel employ the same 'dialectical logic' is to falsify both of them. Marx meant precisely what he said in the 'Afterword' to the second edition of *Capital*: they were 'direct opposites'.

Hegel was no revolutionary, but neither was he the conservative of legend. He was one of those thinkers who tried to illuminate the path of reform in Germany, in response to the French Revolution. After 1819, this path was blocked by the conservative forces in Prussia, and Hegel kept his newly acquired place in the Berlin University Chair of Philosophy only with the greatest difficulty. Some of his students were still less fortunate and ended up in the prisons of the Prussian state.

Like Schiller, Goethe, Schelling, Hölderlin and others in Germany at that time, Hegel tried to grasp the social developments lying in store for Europe. His study of Adam Smith, James Steuart and Adam Ferguson gave him a picture of a world governed by individual self-interest, where the mass of atomised, fragmented human beings was condemned to a life of utterly dehumanising labour. Could the fate which had already overtaken England and Scotland be avoided by their country, and, in any case, what had happened to the promise of the Enlightenment?

The backwardness of Germany gave these thinkers a distinctive angle on such questions. Like the Scots whose work they studied so carefully, they were both inside and outside the developing 'civil society'. Vital for them all was an idealised picture of the ancient Greek *polis*, whose harmony was contrasted with the discord of the modern world. (Hegel saw the need for philosophy as originating in the break-up of this harmony in the fifth century BC.) They were especially impressed by Ferguson, the Gaelic-speaking Highlander, who pointed to parallels between the *polis*, the Highland clans and indigenous North Americans, contrasting them favourably with 'civil society'.

Hegel refused to evade such issues by capitulation to conservatism (like Schelling), an aesthetic and romantic search for another world (Goethe, Schiller), or poetry and madness (Hölderlin). Hegel did not ignore the repulsive forms of nascent bourgeois society which were appearing throughout Europe, but, looking them in the face, tried to reconcile them with the advance of humanity towards freedom.

But how could the discordant forces which were tearing modern society apart be grasped as a united whole? Hegel struggled with this contradiction in every one of his major works. It is not hard to see this in his early writings, or in the *Phenomenology of Spirit*, the *Philosophy of History* and the *Philosophy of Right*. It is less easy to perceive but is nonetheless the unstated question at the heart of the *Logic*. Hegel believed that to answer it was the task of Science ('*Wissenschaft*').

Living with the consequences of nineteenth-century natural science as we do, we can easily misunderstand the term 'science', as it was used by Hegel. The modern scientist is taught to think of himself or herself as an individual operator, living by their privately owned wits and studying objects in an external nature. 'Scientific objectivity' is taken to mean that the thinkers themselves are excluded from the object of study. (I don't have in mind here the ideas of natural scientists themselves, so much as what the philosophers of science tell them they ought to think.)

The procedure known as the 'scientific method' restricts itself from the start by accepting its presuppositions and methods as a matter of faith. To follow it guarantees that you can question neither the meaning of what you are doing, nor the validity of your methods of doing it. Indeed, meaning itself can only be thought of as something external to science, imported subjectively – thus illegally – into the world. Why test that particular hypothesis? Why should failure of a test destroy its truth? What is truth, anyway? Such questions are banned from science and referred to another department.

During the last century, these impoverished forms of thought became widely accepted as the model for all thinking. They show their bankruptcy most plainly when people try to imitate these procedures and attitudes of the natural sciences in those pseudo-sciences called 'social'. 'Marxism', hearing about the transformation of socialism into a science, assumed Marx was some kind of 'social scientist'.

The conceptions of science held by Marx and Hegel, while opposed to each other, are united in rejecting all of this. Hegel spent his life searching for ways to show how, seen correctly, the antagonistic particles which make up modern society could be understood as parts of a whole. But how could he harmonise the cacophonous clash of weapons on 'the battlefield of private interest'?[1] He set himself – and philosophy – a tremendous task. In a world of disunity and oppression, he wanted a science which could grasp human society as organically developing towards unity and freedom. Reflecting on the outcome of the French Revolution, he decided that to be self-determined was only possible in the realm of systematic thought.

Hegel saw science as essentially a *communal* activity and knowledge as a historical process. To engage in scientific work was to participate in the purposive activity of Spirit, the entire movement of History. Only through it could the isolated individual, the inhabitant of 'civil society', get hold of the picture as a whole.

> The task of leading the individual from his uneducated standpoint to knowledge had to be seen in its universal sense, just as it was the universal individual, self-conscious Spirit, whose formative education had to be studied. ... The single individual is incomplete Spirit, a concrete shape in whose whole existence one determinatedness predominates.[2]

Reason was the unifying power in knowledge, described by Hegel as 'purposive activity'.[3] It was not the activity or purpose of any individual thinker which did this work, but the action of Spirit, the subjectivity of an entire social organism. This is what Hegel means when he says: 'Everything turns on grasping and expressing the True, not only as *Substance*, but equally as *Subject*.'[4]

Such knowledge could not base itself on individual opinions, as Hegel explained in his very first lecture in Berlin: 'An opinion [*Meinung*] is *mine*, it is not an inherently universal absolute. ... Philosophy is an objective science of truth, a science of its necessity, of conceptual knowing; it is no opining and no web-spinning of opinions.'[5] Philosophical science was not spun out of the heads of great thinkers, but was rooted in all the life and work of the whole of humanity.

> The possession of self-conscious rationality, a possession belonging to us, to our contemporary world, has not been gained suddenly. ... It is essentially an inheritance and ... the result of labour, the labour of all the preceding generations of the human race. The arts of the externals of our life, the mass of means and skills, the arrangements and customs of social and political associations, all these are the result of the reflection, invention, needs, misery and misfortune, the will and achievement of the history which has preceded our life of today.[6]

What science must achieve is not just knowledge of something outside us, but *self*-knowledge, where 'self' refers to the entire spiritual collective. It was at once a subjective and an objective activity, tracing the path taken by the past movement of Spirit, but *only* the past. The method of this science, logic, was itself a science, and thus a part of History. It revealed the pattern of inner connections which bind reason into a unity. Reason was not a set of external rules to be followed by correct thinking, nor was logic a kind of calculus, merely pointing to the formal links between the forms of objects. The forms were inseparable from their content. The logical structure of Hegel's science had to demonstrate how its objects were *necessarily* connected. 'Logic being the science of the absolute form, this formal science, in order to be *true*, must possess in its own self a *content* adequate to its form.'[7]

A logical judgement – 'the rose is red', 'Socrates is a man' – appears to be an assertion that the subject and object are judged *by us* to have some relationship. But, Hegel believed, in his account of Being and Essence he had demonstrated they belonged together *essentially*. The judgement necessarily gives rise to the syllogism, which itself, through the development of its 'figures', shows how it embodies truth.

The criterion for truth, insisted Hegel, could not be external to systematic knowledge. It was not a matter of showing that the assertions of science were 'correct', by holding them up against some image of a reality external to them, or testing them by applying a rule for correctness. Truth had to be found in the very categories of thought, developed within the system itself.

> Hitherto, the Notion of logic has rested on the separation ... of the *content* of cognition and its *form*, or of *truth* and *certainty*. ... [I]t is assumed that the material of knowing is present on its own account as a ready-made world apart from thought, that thinking on its own is empty and comes as an external form to the said material, fills itself with it and only thus acquires a content and so becomes real knowing.[8]

To do the job Hegel set it, science had to be organically unified, a living system, which contained its own presuppositions and its own method of development within itself. It did not try to answer questions which were posed from outside, but only those questions which were generated by its own workings. It had to include itself in its conception of the world. And it had to be dynamic, self-developing through continual self-criticism, grasping the contradictions, not just between itself and something outside it, but within its own body.

When it encounters such contradictions,

> [t]hinking will not give up, but remains faithful to itself even in this loss of its being at home with itself, 'so that it may overcome', and may accomplish in thinking itself the resolution of its own contradictions.[9]

So Hegel's dialectic cannot be a set of formulae or rules to be detached and 'applied' elsewhere. Dialectic means grasping that the contradictions which confront us at every turn are contradictions of the finite, which science is driven to transcend.

That is what everything finite is: its own sublation [*Aufhebung*]. Hence, the dialectical constitutes the moving soul of scientific progression, and it is the principle through which alone *immanent coherence and necessity* enter into the content of science, just as all genuine, nonexternal elevation above the finite is to be found in this principle.[10]

At his most optimistic, in 1816, Hegel told his Heidelberg students:

The courage of truth, faith in the power of the spirit, is the first condition of philosophising. Because man is spirit he should and must deem himself worthy of the highest; he cannot think highly enough of the greatness and power of his spirit. For a man of this faith nothing is so inflexible and refractory as not to disclose itself to him. The original hidden and reserved essence of the universe has no force which could withstand the courage of knowing [*Erkennens*]; it must expose itself to that courage, bring its wealth and depths to light for our enjoyment.[11]

Was Hegel an idealist? Does this question refer to a belief that the world was a product of an individual mind, like Berkeley; or that the way we got to know it had to begin with the certainty of the individual 'I', like Descartes; or that we constructed our picture of it by means of individually-possessed categories (Kant)? Then the answer is a decided no! *That* kind of idealism, said Hegel, was 'a pure *assertion* which does not comprehend its own self, nor can it make itself comprehensible to others'.[12]

Hegel claims, however, that *his* kind of idealism is shared by any real philosophy. It is basically the idea that truth cannot be found in isolated bits and pieces, but belongs only to the whole picture.

The proposition that the finite is ideal [ideell] constitutes idealism. The idealism of philosophy consists in nothing else than in recognising that the finite has no veritable being. Every philosophy is essentially an idealism, or at least has idealism for its principle. ... Consequently, the opposition of idealism and realistic philosophy has no significance.[13]

This ideality of the finite is the most important proposition of philosophy, and for that reason every genuine philosophy is *Idealism*.[14]

However 'mystical' it is made to appear in many standard accounts, the shape of Hegel's system is the direct and precise expression of the task he set philosophy to perform. He is convinced that systematic thinking is the only way that the unity and development of the world can be grasped. The demand that his science be absolute, that is, independent of anything external to it, determines Hegel's conception of Nature, and its relation to Spirit.

Estranged from the Idea, Nature is only the corpse of the Understanding.[15]

Nature exhibits no freedom in its existence, but only necessity and contingency.[16]

Nature, even at the highest point of its elevation over finitude, always falls back into it again and in this way exhibits a perpetual cycle.[17]

Most striking is Hegel's inability to conceive of anything like historical development in Nature, including the evolution of organisms.[18]

Now let us briefly illustrate Hegel's approach to social problems with a couple of examples of the way that his dialectic copes with them.

The problem of crime and punishment is one to which he gave considerable attention. He defines crime as 'the initial use of coercion, as force employed by a free agent in such a way as to infringe the existence of freedom in its concrete sense – ie to infringe right as right'.[19] In his attitude to the punishment of a criminal act, Hegel is quite liberal. For example, he is for only limited use of the death penalty. While he believes strongly in capital punishment for murder, he is critical of its imposition in England at that time for theft. The idea of punishment as revenge, as a preventative, as a deterrent or corrective, all leave him cold.

Crime is an infringement of 'right as right', and punishment is the 'cancellation' of this infringement. What matters to Hegel is neither the injury to the victim nor the distortion of the criminal, but the contradiction between the crime and the logical whole. Crime has the logical status of the 'negative infinite judgement', like saying 'a lion is not a table' – correct but pointless. It affirms the total incommensurability of subject and predicate.[20]

Someone who commits a crime – for argument's sake a theft – does not merely deny the particular right of someone else to this particular thing (as in a suit about civil rights); instead, he denies the rights of that person completely; therefore he is not merely obliged to return the thing he stole, but is punished as well, because he has violated right as such, ie right in general.[21]

Hegel is quite aware that the prevalence of crime is to be attributed to the conditions of life to which millions of people are condemned. He even had an inkling that there might be a connection between this phenomenon and the rise of 'civil society'. For him, all of this is quite irrelevant. He is concerned only with the relation of crime to the logical structure of society. He can have no conception that the collision between the criminal and his victim's property rights reflects only one aspect of the inhuman character of private property itself.

Hegel is certain that poverty as a modern phenomenon is the necessary consequence of civil society and is inseparable from the heaping up of wealth at the other pole. He also admits that he knows no solution to this 'problem' which has deplorable results.

[C]ivil society affords a spectacle of extravagance and misery as well as of the ethical corruption common to both.[22]

When a large mass of people sinks below the level of a certain standard of living – which automatically regulates itself at the level necessary for a member of the society in question, that feeling of right, integrity and honour which comes from supporting oneself by one's own activity and work is lost. This leads to the creation of a *rabble* [*Pöbel*], which in turn makes it much easier for wealth to be concentrated in a few hands. ...

... Poverty in itself does not reduce people to a rabble; a rabble is created only by the disposition associated with poverty, by inward rebellion against the rich, against society, the government, etc. ... This in turn gives rise to the evil that the rabble do not have sufficient honour to gain their livelihood through their own work, yet claim they have a right to receive their livelihood. ... The important question of how poverty can be remedied is one which agitates and torments modern societies.[23]

There is no doubt that Professor Hegel was genuinely sorry for poor people. But he could not allow this to determine his philosophical consideration of the problem. As he says, it is not poverty 'in itself' that causes trouble, but the effect it has on the feelings about society of both poor and rich. Hegel refuses to ignore the problem of 'the rabble', or to avoid the awkward way this uncivil entity threatens the equilibrium of civil society. But his attention has to be focussed sternly on the ability of dialectic to accommodate poverty within the overall conception of the movement of History towards freedom. The state sublated the difficulties of civil society, and this was a logical result.

Hegel's project is quite magnificent, and, if you want to make sense of the world of civil society, it is indeed absolutely necessary. It also happens to be utterly impossible to achieve. For to complete it would mean to show how the forms of bourgeois society are compatible with freedom – and they are not. By 1831, when Hegel died, these social forms could already be seen to be forms of oppression. However, what had begun to bring this home to many people in Europe was not some new philosophical argument, but the revolt of the new 'slaves' themselves.

In 1839, when Karl Marx was beginning work on his doctoral dissertation, he recognised Hegel as 'our great teacher'. Thirty-four years later he could still 'avow' himself 'a pupil of that mighty thinker'.[24] But as a postgraduate student, he could already see that the Hegelian School was breaking up.

It was not a matter of some errors in the argument. What was wrong was that

> philosophy has sealed itself off to form a consummate, total world. … The world confronting a philosophy total in itself is … a world torn apart. This philosophy's activity therefore also appears torn apart and contradictory.[25]

In his dissertation itself, in 1841, Marx analysed the positions of the two wings of this school – and accepted neither.[26] The problem for Marx, then and always, was how the knowledge gained in philosophical work could 'turn outwards to the world'.

In 1843, spurred on by the work of Feuerbach, but already going far beyond it, Marx began his first assault on the edifice of the Hegelian system, his *Critique of the Hegelian Philosophy of Law*. He had no quarrel with Hegel's description of the modern state, which was in any case not a justification of Prussian authoritarianism, as the legend has it, but an account of what a rationally reformed Prussia might look like: 'Hegel is not to be blamed for depicting the nature of the modern state as it is, but for presenting that which is as the *nature of the state*.'[27] Marx objects to Hegel's logical approach, the false relation he assumes between his scientific exposition and the world it is supposed to be illuminating.

> The concrete content, the actual definition, appears as something formal; the wholly abstract formal definition appears as the concrete content. The essence of the definitions of the state is not that they

are definitions of the state, but that in their most abstract form they can be regarded as logical metaphysical definitions. Not the philosophy of law but logic is the real centre of interest. Philosophical work does not consist in embodying thinking in political definitions, but in evaporating the existing political definitions into abstract thoughts. Not the logic of the matter, but the matter of logic is the philosophical element. The logic does not serve to prove the state, but the state to prove the logic.[28]

Hegel has turned upside-down the relation between philosophy and the world, says Marx. Hegel's method reflects the upside-down, inhuman, irrational way that people live, and in so doing attempts to make it appear as the embodiment of reason.

Marx's theoretical and practical work over the next four decades unfolded the implications of this 'inversion' of the relationship of science to the world. By the start of 1844, in the Introduction to the *Critique of the Hegelian Philosophy of Law* – the only part he ever completed – Marx had begun to see that he was looking for the way to 'actualise philosophy', and that this demanded a social power of a special kind.

As philosophy finds its *material* weapons in the proletariat, so the proletariat finds its *spiritual* weapons in philosophy. And once the lightning of thought has struck this ingenuous soil of the people, the emancipation of the *Germans* into *human beings* will take place.[29]

Both his study of political economy and his conception of communist revolution, which engaged Marx's attention for the rest of his life, began from there. He saw the three great achievements of bourgeois thought as being political economy, Hegel's dialectic and utopian socialism. These three took the attempt of individual thinkers to grasp the atomised modern world as a totality as far as it could go. In his scientific critique of them, Marx showed that all three of them unconsciously expressed the inhumanity of the world they studied.

Where Hegel's science strove to reconcile the conflicting forces of the modern world, Marx's science set out from the necessity to actualise those very conflicts and bring them to fruition. For instance, if science showed that the state expressed the contradictions of 'civil society' founded on private property, this told us that both private property and the state were unfit for human life, and had to be abolished.

Hegel's dialectic had locked up all the disintegrating forces of modern life into a system of concepts, while Marx's science struggled to *unlock* them. Obviously, then, the latter could never be a closed *system*. It was *in principle* incomplete, open. Marx's science could only do its job when it went beyond the bounds of science as such. Its problems could neither be posed nor solved on the level of knowledge.

The key category of Marx's theoretical work was the one which 'Marxism' sought to evade: the idea of 'humanness'. Without it, notions like 'capital', 'proletariat' and 'surplus value' have no meaning. His standpoint, that of *'human society or socialised humanity'* (*Theses on Feuerbach*, Thesis 10),[30] enabled Marx to understand that certain forms of human life were beneath the dignity of *homo sapiens*, not 'worthy and appropriate for their human nature'.[31]

But hidden inside these very forms was a human content, which science had to discover. Within the framework of individualism, inside which men and women had to fight each other to live, they retained, perhaps only in odd corners of their beings, their potential for self-determination, self-creation, self-consciousness and social solidarity. Indeed, it was only because there was a mismatch between this humanity and its inhuman forms, and because people had to struggle to 'fight out' this discrepancy, that it was possible to know which way up the world should go.

Any account of any part of Marx's work which does not centre on this conception – and that includes 90 per cent of the huge volume of writings on the subject – must be utterly false. It seems to me that the supreme task today, and not an easy one, is to disinter Marx's fundamental insight, and to find ways to articulate it in as accessible a form that we can, free of all academic mystification. Only then can it become the foundation for practical action. It was his conception of 'humanness' which gave Marx his criterion for truth. For example:

> The mediating process between men engaged in exchange is not a social or human process, not *human* relationship; it is the abstract relationship of private property to private property. ... Since men engaged in exchange do not relate to each other as men, *things* lose the significance of human personal property.[32]

To identify Hegel's dialectic with the method of Marx is to deny such a view. For Hegel's conception of science left no room for such a critical judgement – indeed, it was designed especially to preclude it. Humanity, identified as Spirit, just *was*, and there was nothing more to be said about it. Hegel believed that science had to comprehend the forms taken by human life and consciousness, not to ask 'should they be', but only to show the necessary place of each as a part of the whole picture. This is what Marx meant when he referred to

the kind of consciousness – and philosophical consciousness is precisely of this kind – which regards the comprehending consciousness [*begreifende Denken*] as the real man, and the comprehended world as such as the real world.[33]

That is why Hegel could consider neither the state nor political economy as subjects for critique. He could only pay tribute to the scientific work of Smith, Say and Ricardo. Marx was also an admirer of these great thinkers. But he saw that when they viewed human society as a collection of individuals inspired by self-interest, they were accurately reflecting the real relations of bourgeois society, and making them appear as if this were the 'natural' way to live.

The understanding of what is and what is not human permeates Marx's conception of science. Consider two well-known remarks from Volume 3 of *Capital*: '[A]ll science would be superfluous if the form of appearance [*Erscheinungsform*] of things and their essence [*Wesen*] directly coincided.'[34] And earlier, discussing 'prices of production':

In competition, therefore, everything appears upside-down. The finished configuration [*Gestalt*] of economic relations, as these are visible on the surface, in their actual existence [*realen Existenz*], and therefore also in the notions [*Vorstellungen*] with which the bearers and agents of these relations seek to gain an understanding of them, is very different from the configuration of their inner core, which is essential [*wesentlichen*] but concealed [*verhüllten*], and the concept [*Begriff*] corresponding to it. It is in fact the very reverse and antithesis of this.[35]

Here, the parallels between Marx's method and Hegel's are plain to see. But only in Marx's case is a further question immediately raised (although rarely by 'Marxists'): *why* are appearance and essence opposed? Why can't we live in such a way that they *do* coincide? His struggle to answer such questions is the heart and soul of Marx's critique of political economy, of his conception of history and of his notions of the communist revolution and communist society.

When 'Marxism' thought that Marx had produced a set of 'economic doctrines', a 'Marxist political economy', and when it identified 'Marx's dialectic' with Hegel's dialectic, it was denying Marx's central insight. In presenting the most developed form of his work on the critique of political economy, in the 1873 edition of *Capital*, Marx explained quite clearly that 'my dialectic is not only different from that of Hegel, but its direct opposite'. Unfortunately, nobody was listening.

Right at the start of his study of political economy, Marx wrote:

> The *community of men*, or the manifestation of the nature of *men*, their mutual complementing the result of which is species-life, truly human life – this community is conceived by political economy in the form of *exchange* and *trade*. ... It is seen that political economy *defines* the *estranged* form of social intercourse as the *essential* and *original* form corresponding to man's nature.[36]

In opposition to this, Marx knew that

> since *human* nature is the *true community* of men, by manifesting their *nature* men *create*, produce, the *human community*, the social entity, which is no abstract universal power opposed to the single individual, but is the essential nature of each individual, his own activity, his own life, his own spirit, his own wealth.[37]

As he put it nearly thirty years later:

> The categories of bourgeois political economy ... are forms of thought which are socially valid, and therefore objective, for the relations of production belonging to this historically determined mode of social production. ...
>
> These formulas, which bear the unmistakeable stamp of belonging to a social formation in which the process of production has mastery over man, instead of the opposite, appear to the political economists' consciousness to be as much a self-evident and nature-imposed necessity as productive labour itself.[38]

Marx's critique of political economy cannot be separated from his critique of the Hegelian dialectic.[39] He showed how Hegel's logic expressed most profoundly the logic of money and capital, and was bound up with the distortion, inversion and inhumanity of the forms of consciousness through which money operated. For Hegel, as for Ricardo, money simply functioned as a 'universal means of exchange', promoting justice and equality.[40]

Marx, by analysis of the categories of the political economists themselves, showed how this relation's impersonal power arose necessarily out of the nature of the commodity and enslaved the whole of society, both rich and poor. The *substance*, 'value', transformed itself into the active *subject*, 'capital', and this was what Hegel unconsciously depicted as 'Spirit'.[41] Where Hegel sees Spirit as the product of human social activity which controls our lives, Marx sees capital.

When Marx unfolds the forms of value, their necessary development into the money-form and the development of money into capital, he deliberately refers to Hegel's exposition of the Judgement and the Syllogism. Hegel's account shows no way out of the inexorable forward march of the Idea. Marx points to the inhumanity and craziness (*Verrücktheit*) of these forms, whose apparent 'inevitability' and 'naturalness' he shows to arise from within this inhuman social formation itself.

So these parallel logical processes actually move in opposite directions. Hegel purports to demonstrate that thought can find a place for all kinds of phenomena of the modern world. Anything, indeed, that is to be discovered existing there has to be shown to be there of necessity. However miserable people may be in such situations, they will be consoled when they hear how it is all for the best 'in the end'. The dialectic moves on past their misery, majestically carrying 'us' – 'we who look on' – to the heights of the Absolute.

In Marx, on the contrary, the forms demonstrate in their movement the way the dialectical trick works. They show us, step by step, *how* the inhuman relations inside which we live our lives disguise themselves as 'natural'. This is the direct opposite of his 'great master'. Hegel locks the gates of our inhuman prison, fixing to them the sign 'Freedom'. Marx wants to show us, not just that we are imprisoned, certainly not a utopian picture of what lies beyond the walls, but how we locked ourselves in and thus *how to get out*, that is, to live as humans.

Was Karl Marx a materialist? If this word is used to mean something about 'matter being given to us through our senses', or thinking being a 'reflection of matter', certainly not. Such materialism, said Marx, took the standpoint of 'the isolated individual in civil society' (*Theses on Feuerbach*, Thesis 10).[42] When he called himself a materialist, he wanted to stress how scientific thinking reflected 'the real movement': 'Technology reveals the active relation of man to nature, the direct production process of his life.'[43] But bourgeois society turned technology and natural science into instruments for the inhuman exploitation of both Nature and labour-power. This is the root cause of 'the weaknesses of the abstract materialism of natural science, a materialism which excludes the historical process'.[44]

By liberating society from fetishised forms, the communist revolution would make it possible for humanity to see its true relationship with Nature. Productive activity was revealed as 'a process between man and nature', in which the human being 'confronts the materials of nature as a force of nature'. When a human being 'acts upon nature and changes it ... he simultaneously changes his own nature' and 'develops the potentialities slumbering within nature'. That is why Marx's science – in direct opposition to Hegel's – could see the potentially human role of the natural sciences:

> History itself is a *real* part of *natural history* – of nature developing into man. Natural science will incorporate into itself natural science: there will be *one* science ... The *social* reality of nature, and *human* natural science, or the *natural science of man*, are identical terms.[45]

Marx could not have done his job without Hegel. By exhibiting the workings of his dialectic in such detail and so comprehensively, Marx's 'great teacher' had given us a faithful map of our jail. All that Marx needed to do was to turn the map upside-down and reverse the arrows on the signposts. That is why *critique*, in the special meaning Marx gave that term, was so important for Marx's work. Through gaps and internal contradictions in Hegel's system, Marx could glimpse possible routes for our escape tunnel.

Of course, just as Hegel's task could never be completed, Marx's was also one that could never have an end. In any case, he only had time to begin the study of one particular item on his agenda. If we refuse to be bound by the false notion of 'Marxism', the idea that it possessed the patent on a 'complete, integral world-outlook', then we stand a chance of following Marx's lead and continuing his work into the uncharted terrain of the twenty-first century.

5   Some Questions for the Twenty-first Century

In place of the old bourgeois society, with its classes and class antago-
nisms, we shall have an association in which the free development
of each is the condition for the free development of all.[1]

Introduction

In the 'Marxist' tradition, it was customary to end a book with a
rousing answer to the question: 'What is to be done?' Maybe the day
for conclusions like that will return some time, but I certainly don't know
how to provide one now. Instead, I shall take a rather tentative look
at a few of the problems which beset the world at the end of the
century, and see if the ideas of Karl Marx can help us to formulate them.

None of these questions are easily answered. However, if it is thought
that humanity is a network of computers, or that each human being is
a survival machine for some bits of DNA, they are absolutely insoluble.
Each of them involves some aspect of the barrier which stands between
human beings and their humanity, that is, the control of their own lives.
In each case, this denial of humanity is itself the result of human
activity, and so a distorted form of that very potential for self-consciousness and self-creation which *is* humanity.

It is easy to see what is *not* to be done. There have been too many
attempts at 'social engineering' – people who know what is good for
us trying to impose answers on us. Humanity implies freedom, sociality
and self-consciousness. The achievement of a human society must itself
be the outcome of free, conscious activity, involving profound alterations in the way billions of people think about each other and about
themselves.

Marx's scientific work aimed to pose such questions in a shape in
which they could be answered in practice – one reason why this work
could never be completed. Once it is grasped that the truth about
humanity is concealed by the collective activity of humanity itself, it is
possible to ask what stands in the way of a 'truly human society'.

Today's list of problems must include many items which Marx himself never encountered. So it is obvious that he could not provide ready-made answers to the questions of the twenty-first century, or even those of the nineteenth and twentieth. It is no good looking for recipes for a better way of life. However, you might get a clearer understanding of the tasks which the species must collectively work to accomplish.

But what can be meant by 'collective work'? For each of the issues I raise in this chapter, it turns out that, from the standpoint of the 'single individual in civil society', the phrase has no meaning at all. Each problem is the outcome of the activity of the whole of society and its solution can only be found by us all.

Neither utopianism nor cynicism can see what Marx saw so clearly: the potential for a human way of living is already in being. Marx's communism was not a utopian vision, but the realisation of possibilities which are already here, the human potential hidden inside our inhuman existence. Marx's question was: how are we we to become what we already are?

That transformation means altering many different aspects of human life at the same time. Attempts to change this or that particular feature must inevitably fail. Although, in the following pages, I will look at specific aspects individually, it is important to bear in mind that each one is bound up with all of the others.

Technology and the Market

Compare the technical powers now available to our species with those of only a few decades ago, and you will see how much things have changed, and how enormous has been the speed of change. In the last twenty years, the advance in productive capacity and speed of communication has affected almost every part of the globe.

But *is* it an advance, and where is it taking us? For example, when people talk about the 'economic development' of parts of the world which seem not to have enjoyed it as yet, what do they really mean? Just look at the consequences of being 'developed' for some of these countries: they have often been as bad as the underdevelopment which was being cured. And in the 'advanced' countries, has technology and industrialisation proved such a wonderful thing? The plight of millions of people shows otherwise.

How can this be? Isn't technology the means to liberate us from the burden of labour? If each application of scientific knowledge is the outcome of the work of the entire human race, why does it increasingly fragment and impoverish our lives? Is this outcome of technological advance inherent in the nature of machines?

We might think we use machines, but we are mistaken: in their form as elements of capital, *they* use *us*. The life of a producer must be twisted to conform to the needs of the machine, while the shape, operation and use of the machine is determined by the impersonal workings of the market. Marx showed how this reversal overtook us. Each human was transformed into a 'personification' of one of the conflicting elements of capital. Relations between them were fixed as if they were acting out these roles from a script.

Among our other shortcomings, we 'Marxists' did not take enough notice of the extent and speed of the advance in productive capacity in recent decades, or ask what changes these implied. Combining the satisfaction of the needs of the world's population with a reduced expenditure of effort seemed to socialists of older generations to be a massive task. It has now become quite a modest aim.

Looked at in terms of technique alone, there really is no necessity for hunger or homelessness in the world, and that has been true for a long time. Shortages of material goods only express a tremendous waste of effort and resources. A huge proportion of the labour carried out in the industrialised countries is directed to quite useless ends, if 'usefulness' is measured in human terms. People are chiefly engaged in keeping capital gainfully employed. In other countries, millions of lives are used up in the most inefficient methods of labour, while millions more are unemployed.

Of course, in a world where money rules and consciousness is gripped by financial psychosis, such questions can *not* be seen in terms of technique. For example: what is the 'best' way to make cars? Is it any use asking about how many cars it is possible to make, without thinking about their relationship to the way humans live? Who will buy them? If we increase the rate of production, what does this mean for those who make them, for their future livelihood and their future lives? What happens to those who used to make them, but are no longer needed? When those cars are driven, what effect will their exhaust fumes have? How will their future owners feel about them, and about other car-owners?

In every part of the world, the new technology has made its mark on all our lives through the same medium: the market on which goods and 'services' are globally bought and sold. It has become fashionable lately to take it for granted that we just cannot live without 'the market'. The global system of production, we are always being told, has become so complicated that we have to allow the wonderful 'market mechanism' to organise productive relations for us and to distribute the resulting wealth. The only alternative, they say, is oppressive bureaucratic direction.

To rely on the invisible hand of 'market forces' to arrange things for us is to assume that the productive activities of five billion individuals can only be linked by setting them against each other, each fragment fighting for his or her own 'interest'. Marx's insight into the implications of exchange-relationships is vital to grasp what all this means. He showed how exchanging commodities led necessarily to the emergence of money, and that money grew into capital.

Not only did the owners of capital exploit the labour of their employees, but capital as an impersonal power came to dominate the whole of world society. If society is seen from the standpoint of the isolated individual – and this way of thinking is continually hammered into our heads by this very way of living – it is impossible to see it for what it is.

'The market' is not a neutral 'medium' at all. Human powers and human needs appear in the mystified forms of the powers and needs of capital. Look at a plant making those cars, at the machines, the activities of those who work on them and the cars they turn out. These don't exist only as material entities and processes. More important is their *social* being, and these two aspects are in general *opposed* to each other. They are all subsumed under the needs and laws of capital, beyond the control of any human consciousness.

The parasitic capital which predominates today, controls us in the shape of finance, involving the movement of credit. When Marx wrote about the first signs of the development of this kind of capital in the 1860s, he referred to 'all manner of insane forms'.[2] But perhaps he could not imagine just how crazy these forms could get.

Surplus-value, extracted from the labour of wage-workers, is the ultimate source of all the immense wealth of the financier of today. It flows from this source along all kinds of intricate paths: interest, commissions, bribes, tax evasion, share dealing, currency speculation, commodity trading, and so on. These manipulations of financial instruments, and the many and varied kinds of lying and cheating through which they operate, are increasingly remote from the production going on in factories. It is almost impossible to disentangle the channels through which they control the lives of each of us, as impossible for those in charge as for the rest of us.

Marx showed the source of the resulting mystification of economic relations. But, over the last few decades, this mystery has deepened enormously, and the implications of the leap in technology which has gone on in the same period have been concealed from us. Once again, our own actions affect us in ways which are out of control.

Industry provides the potential for the liberation of humanity from drudgery and monotony. What changes are needed, in the relationships between us and the ways we see those relationships, for that potential to be released? About fifty years ago, there was much talk of 'automation' and how it would lead to the reduction of the working week. In the 1980s there was a lot of chatter about 'post-industrial society'.

In practice, introducing the new technology has brought about the two-tier labour market. People in the growing lower layer are trapped by poor education and inner-city housing either in long-term unemployment or in degrading and mindless forms of work. The official response is a combination of indifference and utopian chatter about an 'economic recovery'. At the upper level, people in high-tech occupations, driven by the search for money, are desperately busy performing tasks of less and less meaning. In each case, technology encased in the market acts to dehumanise life and to destroy it.

And yet, even with the existing level of technology, there is no need for either poverty or for drudgery to persist. The technical possibilities already exist for the machines to be made to fit *human* needs, rather than the other way round, and for the opposition between working and living to begin to fade. Then we could realise the possibilities locked inside the market-controlled technology. Everything turns on understanding what humans and their needs *are*.

On the other hand, if we don't break technology out of its market shell, it is powerful enough to destroy us. At the end of the second millennium, we have no choice. The inhuman forms of life which surround us all threaten our very survival. Unless we escape and liberate our true humanity, they will strangle us.

Technology and the Natural Environment

That the rise of modern industry has been disastrous for the natural environment has been known for a long time. In the 1960s the extent of these effects began to show themselves. Some side-effects of industrialism started to worry some people. There was much discussion about a 'population explosion': more humans were being born and surviving than the world could hold. The earth's natural resources were being used up. Complex, naturally evolved systems of living organisms were being thrown out of balance. Species of organisms were disappearing fast.

Of course, we 'Marxists' tended to brush aside the 'Green' movement's concerns, declaring that these were just by-products of the drive for private profit. We were sure that central planning of industry would put a stop to all such dangers. The Chernobyl disaster, followed by revelations about the disgraceful environmental record of the Stalinist governments, made this confidence look a bit stupid.

But the Green movements which have developed over the past three decades are marked by enormous confusion. Some Greens accuse Marx of favouring 'human domination of nature', which they say is evil. There is much talk of 'animal rights' and the 'rights' of nature generally, of 'our responsibility to nature', of the inherent destructiveness of *homo sapiens*.

I don't see how you can speak about 'rights', except in terms of *human* responsibility. How can individuals be *responsible* for a situation where individual action is meaningless and where there is no way to act collectively? Does human destructiveness deny its ability to create? Behind the attitude of the ecologically minded, you can often see peeping out the idea that technology itself is a Bad Thing, and behind that, sometimes, the not very sensible notion that the world would be a better place without humanity. (This is actually the stated view of the self-styled 'deep ecologists'.)

Environmental issues are often expressed as if these were a choice between an environmentally sound policy and higher living standards. Such arguments are always based on the assumption that the existing economic set-up, or something like it, is here to stay. Greens seem to blame the modest living standards of ordinary people in industrialised countries for environmental dangers. Where does this leave the countries which have not yet industrialised? There is sometimes an appeal to masochism which can give 'Green' rhetoric a nasty authoritarian flavour, a characteristic it shares with a lot of utopianism.

Humanity is a part of nature, certainly, but *what* part? As the self-conscious, self-creating outcome of natural evolution, only socialised humanity provides the standpoint from which nature can be understood and assessed. This includes understanding the necessity to look after the natural environment on which human life depends. To live humanly, conscious that we create ourselves socially as part of nature, must imply that we treat the world around us in a way which protects our present and future well-being. That is the only sensible criterion for the 'well-being' of nature.

I can see no inherent reason why technological development has to be damaging to the eco-system. Freed from the dead hand of the market mechanism, it could be directed to providing for the satisfaction of the needs of everybody, and, properly understood, that includes the avoidance of ecological destruction. On this basis, instead of trying to make people feel guilty that they are consuming too much, it becomes possible to show them what collective actions are needed to look after the well-being of us all.

Industry and the State

'Marxists', and indeed many other sorts of socialist, were really hung up on the idea of central planning. Instead of the anarchy of privately owned industrial enterprises, each following its own agenda, we wanted to see the state centrally deciding what would be made and how it would be allocated in the community.

We thought that the problem was the 'class nature' of the state, its relationship with the ruling class. Once this class had been got out of the way, either expropriated or bought off, the state would first represent the working masses and then 'wither away'. Life has proved that things were not so simple. There has been a lot of state planning and state intervention everywhere, both 'nationalisation' of the Fabian variety and especially the Stalinist bureaucratic nightmare. We have to stop and think again about this question.

Certainly, private ownership of the means of production and their exploitation for private profit is at the root of all our troubles. But what would 'social ownership' look like? That is not so obvious. If industry is to be directed consciously, how is this consciousness to be achieved and how is it to function?

The state came to act as a false substitute for the community – as Marx said, it was the 'illusory community'. (Lenin glimpsed this after the collapse of the Second International – and then forgot about it.) However 'democratic' the form taken by this machine, it could never be the instrument for human self-creation.

These days, when the national character of the state collides with the global forms of capital, this problem cannot be avoided. Moreover, while I used to think that the state should regulate economic life, we now see that every government is controlled by the market, which is increasingly beyond the reach of any of them.

In the 1990s, the state in the most important countries is securely tied up with the dominance of parasitic capital, utterly permeated with global money. Its traditional connections with the most powerful sections of capital are less clear than they used to be. Instead, the personnel who actually count in the state, chosen as media personalities or military leaders, often have very personal links with finance. As the last remnants of the old bureaucratic structures of the USSR crumble away, their replacement by 'modern' – that is, financially corrupt – states, exhibit some instructive lessons.

Rather than giving up in depair at these features of the uncontrollability of modern life, we have to see that they demonstrate the impossibility of going on this way. Since the state is an expression of our inhuman life, it is not merely a matter of changing its 'class character'.

Can humans collectively govern themselves? When human productive powers have been freed from the social form of capital, the opposition between society and community can disappear. Relations between 'social individuals' will not be regulated by an unconscious, impersonal, machine-like power, but consciously by the 'associated individuals'.

These are old questions for socialists. As we enter the new millennium, we know that they cannot be evaded, but we also have more experience on which to base our answers.

Feminism

When the feminist movement began to demonstrate that 'the personal is political', 'Marxists' found the notion hard to handle. What had the most personal of relationships got to do with 'laws of history' and 'economic doctrines'? The oppression of women would be overcome through the socialist revolution, and not before, and this was a matter of 'class politics', not personal relations.

I can now see that this was a very narrow-minded attitude. The work of the feminists has important elements to offer communists. There were many attempts to construct a 'Marxist-feminism', but sometimes the result combined the worst aspects of both. By the 1990s, a lot of feminist work has dwindled from a bold attack on the inhuman treatment of one half of humanity by the other, into the trivialised sterility of 'political correctness'. What began as a movement to change the situation of women here and now found itself increasingly adapting to the existing social order, often focussing its attention on a small section of the better-off women in the better-off countries.

It should not have happened like that. Looking at the human race from the angle of some of its most oppressed individuals, the women's movement ought to have made us search out Marx's fundamental ideas from their hiding place inside the 'Marxist' tradition. The importance of forms of oppression which 'Marxism' had ignored might then have been investigated. Shortcomings of Marx himself would have been brought into the open and their correction would have shown the way to deeper insight into what he was trying to do.

Remember that Marx ended his 'criticism of religion' and began his 'criticism of politics' with 'the teaching that man [*Mensch*] *is the highest being for man*, hence with the *categorical imperative to overthrow all relations* in which man is a debased, enslaved, forsaken, despicable being'.[3] It is clear that his fundamental conceptions and the struggle of women for their emancipation must have the deepest relevance for each other. To develop his ideas, we have to see that struggle as a vital part of human emancipation and not to isolate it as a 'women's issue'.

Some tendencies within feminism unfortunately took the centuries-old inhuman treatment of women by men, and tried to turn it upside-down. (This bears some resemblance to 'crude communism', which Marx attacked in 1844, among other reasons because of its reactionary attitude towards women.)

I think that 'Marxism' proved unable to deal with the issue of feminism. In the rediscovery and development of the ideas of Marx, the questions raised by feminism have great importance. In particular, the feminists have pointed out the role of power and dominance in social relations, especially with reference to sexuality.

If we could see gender-relations in a broader, human context, then the question arises: what *is* power? What does it mean for one human being to dominate another? Is this something 'natural', given by our biological make-up? What can be said about the relationship between social forms of domination and their psychological expression? Is it possible for human society to exist without such features?

I do not think Marx could possibly have answered all such questions. But I do believe that his penetration of the nature of property and its forms shows the way they might be tackled.

Racism, Nationalism and Other Horrors

As we check the ideas of Marx against the problems of the new millennium, we must never forget that this was the century of Auschwitz.

Perhaps we might add some 'lesser' monstrosities, like Dresden, Hiroshima, the Gulag, My Lai, Shatila and Sabra. Some think this list of horrors of our time – all state-organised, and using the best technology available – puts in question the very notion of a 'truly human society'. The shadow of the Holocaust is the backdrop for all the scepticism and evasion of 'post-modern' moods.

If these questions have been forgotten at all, then the break-up of the USSR and its satellite regimes, and especially the disintegration of Yugoslavia, has refreshed the memory. *Homo sapiens* has seen itself yet again in its most brutal and repulsive forms. Murderous civil wars, fought in the name of 'the nation', have yielded several fresh items for our list, adding the phrase 'ethnic cleansing' to the world's vocabulary. How can the notion of humanity survive such monstrous experiences? It is certainly not easy to answer questions like these, but we must not look away from them. Marx did not answer them in advance, but I believe his idea of humanity points us towards answers.

Humanity must be a unity and there cannot be more than one. That is why, at the end of the century, the appearance of extreme expressions of fragmentation, like nationalism and racism, is so alarming. The trouble does not lie in the idea of 'nations', those specific cultural or linguistic entities which have developed in the course of history. In the eighteenth and nineteenth centuries, this notion played an essential role in the struggle for liberation from the old oppressive regimes. Formation of the nations of Europe and North America was part of the fight to break the might of landowning aristocrats, kings and emperors, and to establish liberty, equality and fraternity.

For those engaged in that struggle, the freedom and independence of one nation did not contradict the freedom and independence of another. Diversity and unity were complementary, not mutually exclusive. In this century, when capital had enslaved the peoples of Asia, Africa and Latin America, the struggle against it has often taken up the slogans of those earlier battles, demanding the right to 'national self-determination'. So my remarks about nationalism in no way detract from the justice of the struggles which still go on against imperialist oppression and the remnants of colonialism.

The 'ism' of nationalism is something quite different. Its essence is to assert that the 'nation' is the basis for the organisation of social life. National*ism* usually centres, not on the liberation of a group of people, but on the oppression or even the destruction of others. Asserting the rights of your group necessarily implies treating the rest as less than human, claiming the right to do what you want with them. Since the state is 'the illusory community', an impersonal power, the fight for a nationalistic state cannot be about the 'true community' at all.

These movements pretend to be motivated by the history of their nation. Usually, this means highlighting or even inventing quite false accounts of episodes of aggression against them from the pages of history. Sometimes they are associated with the foul and stupid lie that nationhood has a biological character, determined by descent, 'blood' or skin pigment. In other versions, ancient religious differences have been unearthed and erected into causes for inter-communal warfare, in which God Almighty, like some divine football hooligan, murderously favours His chosen team against its rivals.

These days, the destructiveness of nationalism provides itself with the latest equipment. While yelling its archaic war cries, it is likely to be equipped with the very latest in high-tech weaponry. It is usually under military leadership, and has close contact with the forces of parasitic capital and of one or other established state power.

There are many who see the cruelty and destructiveness of our time as proof of the inherent evil of human beings. To say that is really to say nothing. Modern technology has certainly increased the scale of inhuman actions, but it has not added anything essentially new to the long story of inhumanity. Marx was talking about the exploitation of child-labour and the modern slavery of the Southern United States when he wrote: 'If money, according to Augier, "comes into the world with a congenital blood-stain on one cheek", capital comes dripping with blood from head to toe, from every pore, with blood and dirt.'[4]

Marx's contribution was to grasp how the horrors of modern slavery and the African slave trade were the inhuman outcome of the activities of humans. This series of actions was explicable as attending the birth of capital. During Marx's own lifetime, both slavery and child-labour were abolished, at least in the 'advanced countries' where they had flourished. The further development of human self-consciousness, he believed, would reveal that the struggles for these advances were steps on the road to the abolition of all forms of exploitation and oppression.

The Holocaust will always – must always – remain in the minds of future generations as a monument to the debasement of human society. But even this industrialised bestiality was the work of humans expressing the self-creating power of humanity in the most perverted, fetishised shapes. Powerful forces still maintain this perversion. In the shape of fascism they did enormous damage, and might do so again.

Under all conditions, while humanity survives, its conflict with its inhuman forms goes on. Since the obscenities of the concentration camps are the work of human beings, albeit dehumanised ones, human beings can erase them. That, it seems to me, is the way that Marx's conceptions can show the way forward.

Socialism and the Labour Movement

For over two centuries, wage-workers have been combining in the fight against the power of capital. Marx was effectively the first to connect this movement with the conception of a truly human way of life. We have seen how the many varieties of 'Marxist' long ago lost sight of Marx's central notion of humanity. Of course, in the 'official' labour movement, the idea of socialism has been adapted to the political life of the bourgeois state, until almost nothing remains of its origins.

Today, the movement is blessed with leaders whose chief preoccupation is their own careers within the existing set-up. The very idea that capital might disappear fills these men and women with as much dread as it does the capitalists themselves. Those rank-and-file workers who keep the movement alive generally limit themselves to purely defensive actions, trying as best they can to protect their past gains in rights and conditions. The main organisations of the movement have little relation with some of the most oppressed and deprived sections of society.

The revolutionaries, utterly determined to eradicate 'capitalism' and its state, saw this task in terms of the construction of a 'party'. This would organise the 'vanguard' of the working class into a centrally organised body, which could win the allegiance of the majority in setting up a 'workers' state'.

The perversion of Marx's ideas by Stalinism had an especially powerful impact in this area, even on those who fought against it. The idea of 'democratic centralism' was turned into to the pernicious notion that the 'correct theory' was the property of the historically chosen group, and especially its 'leadership'. Social change was a mechanical process which these leaders could somehow initiate by an act of will.[5]

Marx himself, of course, never belonged to a 'Marxist party' or anything like it. His understanding of revolution and revolutionary activity concerned the conscious, collective remaking of social relations between people, through their joint action. The impulse for such a change could only come from the way they live now.

It is certain that, in the new century, the socialist project will revive in the thinking of masses of people. The question is, how will that new generation of socialists get to grips with the problems of the new millennium? The aim is not to force the creation of something which has never existed, but to free those forces which already exist, to 'develop potentialities slumbering within'[6] existing social being. The task is to discover, hidden inside the chaos of modern life, the elements of a set of relations between human beings, including their relations with the natural world, which are 'worthy of their human nature'.

Suppose we are in the dark and lost in a maze. There is a well-known and infallible method of escaping: just put the left hand on the wall and keep walking forwards. Occasionally we will hit the end of a blind alley and have to turn round and retrace our steps. But, eventually, we will emerge into the daylight. In humanity's efforts to find its way out of the nightmare world of the twentieth century, the Russian Revolution might be thought of as an excursion down such a blind alley. This heroic attempt to blast a way through the solid rock failed to achieve its objective and turned out to be a gigantic and tragic historical detour, but that could not be known until the attempt was made.

On our way back from this cul-de-sac, moods of disappointment and cynicism are understandable, but we should not succumb to them. Instead of just bemoaning the time we lost, we must try to understand it as a part of the search as a whole, a process which must take more than one lifetime and more than one generation to accomplish. That means carefully and calmly assembling all the lessons we can from that section of our journey towards the light, using them to clarify the next stage.

It is in this spirit that I have been trying to re-examine the ideas of Karl Marx. If we can clear the ground of the errors of the past, it might be possible to extend Marx's work in the context of the problems of the present.

Notes and References

Abbreviations:

Marx
Where possible, I have referred to the *Marx–Engels Collected Works* (London: Lawrence and Wishart, 1975–94). These references are shown as **volume**: page, together with the name of the work when it is readily available elsewhere. Marx's correspondence is referred to by date of letter and name of recipient.

C1 = *Capital*, **Vol. 1** (Harmondsworth: Penguin, 1976).
C3 = *Capital*, **Vol. 3** (Harmondsworth: Penguin, 1981).

Hegel
Phen = *Phenomenology of Spirit*, trans. A.V. Miller (Oxford: Oxford University Press, 1977).
HP = *History of Philosophy* (Introduction), trans. T.M. Knox and A.V. Miller (Oxford: Oxford University Press, 1985).
PR = *Philosophy of Right*, trans. H.B. Nisbet (Cambridge: Cambridge University Press, 1991).
SL = *Science of Logic*, trans. A.V. Miller (London: Allen and Unwin, 1969).
E1 = *Encyclopaedia (Smaller Logic)*, trans. T.F. Geraets *et al.* (Indianapolis: Hackett, 1991).
E2 = *Encyclopaedia (Philosophy of Nature)*, trans A.V. Miller (Oxford: Oxford University Press, 1970).
E3 = *Encylopaedia (Philosophy of Mind)*, trans. W. Wallace/Miller (Oxford: Oxford University Press, 1971).

Others
LCW = V.I. Lenin: *Collected Works* (London: Lawrence and Wishart, 1960–80).
SPW = Georgi Plekhanov: *Selected Philosophical Works* (Moscow: Progress Publishers, 1976).

KMTR = Hal Draper: *Karl Marx's Theory of Revolution*, 4 vols (New York: Monthly Review Press, 1977, 1978, 1986, 1990).

Preface

1 C.S. Smith, 'Individuals and Social Relations', *Fourth International* (January, 1974).
2 C.S. Smith, *Communist Society and Marxist Theory* (London: Index Books, 1988).

1 The Way We Live Now

1 *The Poverty of Philosophy*, 6: 113.

2 How the 'Marxists' Buried Marx

1 Quoted in a letter from Engels to Bernstein, 2–3 November 1892. See *KMTR* II: 6.
2 See B.J. Dobbs, *The Hunting of the Green Lyon: The Foundations of Newton's Alchemy* (Cambridge: Cambridge University Press, 1975), and especially her second book, *The Janus Faces of Genius: The Role of Alchemy in Newton's Thought* (Cambridge: Cambridge University Press, 1991).
3 I. Silber, *Socialism: What Went Wrong? An Inquiry into the Theoretical Sources of the Socialist Crisis* (London: Pluto Press, 1994), is a good example. The author writes as an old militant of the Communist Party of the USA, and tries to investigate the nature of Stalinism. He provides some useful material, but no real examination of Marx's ideas.
4 *SPW* II: 117.
5 *History of the Communist Party of the Soviet Union (Bolsheviks): Short Course* (Moscow: Foreign Languages Publishing House, 1939), p. 105.
6 Quoted in Helena Sheehan, *Marxism and the Philosophy of Science, Vol. 1, The First Hundred Years* (New Jersey: Humanities Press), p. 183.
7 *History*, p. 115.
8 *Ibid.*, p. 114.

9   *Ibid.*, p. 119.

10   *Ibid.*, p. 123.

11   *Ibid.*, p. 126.

12   J. Habermas, 'The Reconstruction of Historical Materialism', in Tom Rockmore, *Habermas on Historical Materialism* (Bloomington: Indiana University Press, 1989).

13   See P. Pomper, *Trotsky's Notebooks 1933–35* (New York: Columbia University Press, 1986).

14   L. Trotsky, *Stalinism and Bolshevism* (London: New Park, 1956), p. 2.

15   L. Trotsky, *Terrorism and Communism* (London: New Park, 1975), pp. 121 and 123.

16   *Ibid.*, pp. 151 and 159.

17   *Ibid.*, p. 177.

18   *C*1: 103.

19   *The State and Revolution*, *LCW* **25**: 385.

20   *The ABC of Communism* (Harmondsworth: Penguin, 1969), para. 5.

21   *Ibid.*, para. 23.

22   *Ibid.*, para. 48.

23   N. Bukharin, *Historical Materialism: A System of Sociology* (Michigan: Ann Arbor, 1969).

24   *LCW* **32**: 24.

25   *LCW* **32**: 48.

26   *Ibid.*

27   G. Lukacs, *History and Class Consciousness* (London: Merlin, 1971).

28   See Douglas Kellner, *Karl Korsch: Revolutionary Theory* (Texas University Press, 1974), p. 46.

29   *Ibid.*

30   *Survey*, No. 47, April 1967, p. 152. I am grateful to Brian Pearce for giving me this reference.

31   Kautsky's work *The Economic Doctrines of Karl Marx* first appeared in German in 1887. It later became very popular in the labour movement, especially in its English translation.

32   See Sheehan, *Marxism*, p. 79.

33   *LCW* **5**: 375, 384–5.

34   *Communist Manifesto*, **6**: 495.

35   Hal Draper, *The Dictatorship of the Proletariat from Marx to Lenin* (New York: Monthly Review Press, 1987). Also the indispensable four volumes of *KMTR*.

36 *1903. Second Congress of the Russian Social-Democratic Labour Party. Minutes* (London: New Park, 1978), p. 168.
37 Trotsky, *Stalin* (London: Panther, 1969), p. 97. Also see P. Pomper, *Trotsky's Notebooks*, p. 83.
38 *1903*, pp. 219–20.
39 *Ibid.*
40 *LCW* **14**: 19.
41 *SPW* **I**: 516, 'For the Sixtieth Anniversary of Hegel's Death'.
42 *Left-Wing Communism, LCW* **32**: 25.
43 Trotsky, *My Life* (Harmondsworth: Penguin, 1975), p. 148.
44 Note 6, in Plekhanov's 1905 edition of Engels's *Ludwig Feuerbach* (Peking: Foreign Languages Press, 1976).
45 *SPW* **II**: 35.
46 *SPW* **I**: 544–5.
47 *SPW* **III**: 212.
48 See *SPW* **II**: 409.
49 In this connection, it is worth noting a remark of Hegel's, arguing that 'matter' for the eighteenth-century materialists is precisely equivalent to the idea of 'God' for the eighteenth-century deists (*Phen*, 340–1).
50 *LCW* **14**: 130.
51 *Ibid.*
52 *LCW* **38**: 180.
53 *Ibid.*, 179.
54 *Ibid.*, 276.
55 Lenin's letter to Kamenev, July 1917.
56 *The Poverty of Philosophy* **6**: 212.
57 *The Poverty of Philosophy* **6**: 504.
58 Letter from Marx to Kugelmann, 12 April 1871.
59 *LCW* **25**: 413–32.
60 *LCW* **25**: 490.
61 Even in *Proletarian Revolution and The Renegade Kautsky, LCW* **28**: 227–325, Lenin's merciless criticism is confined to political issues.
62 *LCW* **32**: 94.
63 Trotsky, *Stalinism and Bolshevism.*
64 *Anti-Dühring*, **25**: 10.
65 *Anti-Dühring*, **25**: 25–6.
66 *Ludwig Feuerbach and the End of Claasical German Philosophy*, **26**: 365–6.
67 *Ibid.*, **26**: 382–3.
68 *Ibid.*, **26**: 383.

69 See *KMTR* **III**, Part 3, for a great deal of information about Marx's relations with Blanqui and Lafargue's role as would-be matchmaker.

70 See *KMTR* **IV**, Chapter 8.

71 Throughout this section, I have drawn a great deal on T. Shanin (ed.), *Late Marx and the Russian Road: Marx and the 'peripheries of capitalism'* (London: Routledge and Kegan Paul, 1983). In addition to the editor's material, it includes important contributions from Wada, Derek Sayer, Corrigan and Sanders. The volume contains the Zasulich letter, Marx's reply and drafts, and other important material.

72 *Das Kapital*, first edition, *Marx-Engels Gesamt Ausgabe*, **II**, **5**, p. 625. The note comes right at the very end of the text.

73 *C1*: 98.

74 *C1*: 876.

75 *Le Capital* (Paris, 1950), Livre 1, Tome 3, p. 156. Added to the end of Chapter XXVII.

76 Marx to Friedrich Sorge, 27 September 1877.

77 Marx to the Editorial Board of *Otechestvenniye Zapiski*, November 1877.

78 See D. Offord, *The Russian Revolutionary Movement in the 1880s* (Cambridge: Cambridge University Press, 1986).

79 S.H. Baron, *Plekhanov, the Father of Russian Marxism* (Stanford: Stanford University Press, 1963), remains the standard biography, but, especially in connection with Plekhanov's theoretical work and its relationship to Marx, it must be read carefully in the light of the other material we have mentioned.

80 See Shanin, *Late Marx and the Russian Road*, pp. 206–9.

81 Marx to Sorge, 5 November 1880.

82 Marx to Jenny Longuet, 11 April 1881.

83 *Ibid.*

84 See Jay Bergman, *Vera Zasulich* (Stanford University Press, 1983).

85 *Ibid.*, pp. 98–9.

86 Marx to Zasulich, 8 March 1881.

87 *Ibid.*

88 *Ibid.*

89 *Communist Manifesto*, Preface to the Russian Edition, **24**: 426.

90 *The Ethnological Notebooks of Karl Marx (Studies of Morgan, Phear, Maine, Lubbock)*, transcribed and edited by Lawrence Krader (Assen: Van Gorcum, 1974).

91 This Preface is to be found in many places. See, for example, **29**: 263.

92 *Histoire de la II International, tomes 6–7*, pp. 110–11. Minkoff Reprint, Geneva, 1977.

93 *Ibid.*

94 First of the *Theses on Feuerbach*, **5**: 5. I have not been able to find a consideration of this *Thesis* in full in any of Plekhanov's works.

3 'The Standpoint of Socialised Humanity'

1 *Tenth Thesis on Feuerbach*, **5**: 5.
2 *Grundrisse*, **28**: 251.
3 *Sixth Thesis on Feuerbach*, **6**: 5.
4 *C1*: 283.
5 *German Ideology*, **5**: 31.
6 *Paris Manuscripts*, **3**: 303.
7 **3**: 295–6.
8 **3**: 336.
9 **3**: 337.
10 *Grundrisse*, **29**: 91.
11 *Ibid.*, **28**: 420.
12 **3**: 299.
13 **3**: 276.
14 **3**: 298.
15 **3**: 300.
16 *Tenth Thesis on Feuerbach*, **5**: 5.
17 *Ninth Thesis on Feuerbach*, **5**: 5.
18 A few examples in *C1*: 92, 103 and 166 (in Chapter 1) and 929 (in Chapter 32).
19 **3**: 295–6.
20 *German Ideology*, **5**: 49.
21 *Third Thesis on Feuerbach*, **5**: 4.
22 *German Ideology*, **5**: 36.
23 *C1*: 175.
24 *C1*: 174–5.
25 *C1*: 169 translates this word as 'absurd'.
26 *C1*: 169.
27 *C1*: 174–5.
28 *C1*: 168.
29 *Grundrisse*, **28**: 94.

30 *C*1: 165–6.
31 **3**: 221.
32 **3**: 225.
33 **3**: 226.
34 *C*1: 178–9, retranslated.
35 *Phen*: 111–12.
36 *C*1: 187, partly retranslated.
37 *Grundrisse*, **28**: 413.
38 *C*1: 174.
39 *C*1: 139.
40 *Grundrisse*, **29**: 504–5.
41 *Wage-Labour and Capital*, **9**: 211.
42 *C*1: 769.
43 *C*1: 134.
44 *C*1: 176.
45 *Grundrisse*, **28**: 411–12.
46 *Ibid.*, **29**: 91.
47 *Ibid.*
48 *Theories of Surplus Value*, **I**: 186. Also **31**: 83.
49 *Theories*, **I**: 387–8. Also **30**: 306–10.
50 *Theories*, **I**: 401. Also **34**: 448.
51 *C*1: 772.
52 *C*3: 913.
53 *C*3: 911.
54 *C*3: 969.
55 *C*3: 517.
56 *C*3: 596.
57 *C*1: 92.
58 *Eighteenth Brumaire of Louis Napoleon*, **11**: 103.
59 *German Ideology*, **5**: 82.
60 *Preface to A Critique of Political Economy*, **29**: 263.
61 For example, *Grundrisse*, **28**: 419. Derek Sayer's book, *The Violence of Abstraction* (Oxford: Blackwell, 1987), is helpful on this point.
62 **29**: 263.
63 *Ibid.*
64 *Ibid.*
65 *Grundrisse*, **28**: 390–1.
66 *Ibid.*, **28**: 101.
67 *Ibid.*, **29**: 210.
68 *Ibid.*, **29**: 91.

69 D. Ricardo, *Principles of Political Economy and Taxation* (Everyman Paperback Edition), Chapter 1, Section VII.

70 *German Ideology*, **5**: 77.

71 **29**: 264.

72 *Grundrisse*, **29**: 133.

73 *The Ethnological Notebooks of Karl Marx (Studies of Morgan, Phear, Maine, Lubbock)*, transcribed and edited with an introduction by Lawrence Krader (Van Gorcum, the Netherlands, 1974).

74 **3**: 198.

75 **5**: 46–7.

76 **5**: 78.

77 **3**: 198.

78 *Grundrisse*, **28**: 420.

79 **4**: 120–1.

80 *Grundrisse*, **28**: 195.

81 *C3*: 927.

82 *Grundrisse*, **29**: 221.

83 *Ibid.*, **28**: 510.

84 As far as I can tell, Marx's only use of the phrase occurs in response to Bakunin's criticisms: 'He should have asked himself: what forms could management functions assume within such a workers' state, if he wants to call it that' (**24**: 520).

85 For some examples, see Vincent Geoghan, *Utopianism and Marxism* (London: Methuen, 1987).

86 *C1*: 171, retranslated.

87 **3**: 227–8.

88 *Grundrisse*, **29**: 210.

89 *Ibid.*, **29**: 94.

90 *Ibid.*, **29**: 90–1.

91 *Ibid.*

92 *C3*: 959.

93 *German Ideology*, **5**: 52.

94 *Ibid.*, **5**: 52–3.

95 *Poverty of Philosophy* **6**: 212.

96 *Civil War in France*, **22**: 331.

97 *Ibid.*

98 *Ibid.*

99 *Ibid.*, **22**: 332.

100 See Note 84.

101 **24**: 519.

4 Science and Humanity

1 **3**: 303–4.
2 *The Poverty of Philosophy*, **6**: 178.
3 *C1*: 103.
4 My friend Towfik Shomar tells me that my idea of what philosophers of science believe is out of date. See his forthcoming PhD
   thesis for an account of what he calls 'phenomenological theory'.
5 Turing's papers are reprinted in *The Philosophy of Artificial Intelligence*, ed. Margaret A. Boden (Oxford: Oxford University Press,
   1989).
6 For some of the background to the AI discussion, see: *The
   Artificial Intelligence Debate: False Starts, Real Foundations*, ed.
   Stephen R. Graubard, (Cambridge: Cambridge University Press,
   1990); J. David Bolter, *Turing's Man: Western Culture in the
   Computer Age* (Harmondsworth: Penguin, 1984); Boden, *Artificial
   Intelligence*; and *The Boundaries of Humanity: Humans, Animals,
   Machines*, eds James J. Sheehan and Morton Sosna, (Berkeley:
   Berkeley University Press, 1991).
7 A. Newell and H. Simon, 'Heuristic Problem Solving: The
   Next Advance in Operations Research', *Operations Research* 6,
   Jan.–Feb. 1958.
8 P.N. Johnson-Laird, *The Computer and the Mind* (Fontana, 1988),
   is the best statement of the case for regarding the mind as a
   machine. G.M. Edelman's *Bright Air, Brilliant Fire: On the Matter
   of the Mind* (Harmondsworth: Penguin, 1993), contains a powerful
   rejection of this case. See also J.-P. Changeux, *Neuronal Man: The
   Biology of Mind* (Oxford: Oxford University Press, 1986).
9 See for example Joseph Weizenbaum, *Computer Power and Human
   Reason* (Harmondsworth: Penguin, 1976), and Terry Winograd,
   'Thinking Machines: Can There Be? Are We?', in Sheehan and
   Sosna (eds), *Boundaries of Humanity*.
10 John Searle, *Minds, Brains and Science: 1984 Reith Lectures* (London:
   BBC Books, 1984), p. 18. However, see John Searle, *Minds, Brains
   and Programs*, in Boden, *Articicial Intelligence*, p. 86:

   'Could a machine think?' My own view is that only a machine
   could think, and indeed *only* very special kinds of machines,
   namely brains and machines that had the same causal powers
   as brains ... AI has had little to tell us about thinking, since it
   ... is about programs, and programs are not machines.

11 *Ibid.*
12 *Minds, Brains and Programs*, p. 84.
13 E.O. Wilson, *Sociobiology: The New Synthesis* (Cambridge, Mass.: Harvard University Press, 1975).
14 *Ibid.*, p. 552.
15 *Ibid.*, p. 561.
16 E.O. Wilson, *On Human Nature* (Cambridge, Mass.: Harvard University Press, 1978), p. 3.
17 *Ibid.*, pp. 5–6.
18 *Ibid.*, p. 95.
19 *Ibid.*, p. 169.
20 R. Dawkins, *The Selfish Gene*, (Oxford: Oxford University Press, 1976), Preface to the new edition.
21 *The Adapted Mind: Evolutionary Psychology and the Generation of Culture*, eds J.H. Barkow, L. Comides and John Tooby (Toronto: Toronto University Press, 1989).
22 *The Code of Codes: Scientific and Social Issues in the Human Genome Project*, eds D.J. Kevles and L. Hood, (Cambridge, Mass.: Harvard University Press, 1992), p. 96. For a discussion, see R.C. Lewontin's *The Doctrine of DNA. Biology as Ideology* (Harmondsworth: Penguin, 1993).
23 For an authoritative opposition to the 'orthodox' view, see Brian Goodwin's *How the Leopard Changed its Spots: The Evolution of Complexity* (London: Weidenfeld and Nicolson, 1994).
24 See *The Sociobiology Debate: Readings on the Ethical and Scientific Issues Concerning Sociobiology*, ed. Arthur J. Caplan, with a foreword by Edward O. Wilson (New York: Harper, 1978).
25 Steven Rose, R.C. Lewontin and Leon J. Kamin, *Not in Our Genes: Biology, Ideology and Human Nature* (Harmondsworth: Penguin, 1984).
26 *C*1: 151–2.
27 *C*3: 956.
28 *C*1: 169.
29 *C*1: 729–30.
30 *C*1: 102.
31 **28**: 37.
32 Hiroshi Uchida, *Marx's Grundrisse and Hegel's Logic* (London: Routledge, 1989).
33 I am indebted to Ute Bublitz for the discussion of translations of Marx, here and throughout the book.
34 **28**: 37.

35   This passage of *Grundrisse* raises a problem: did Marx think that
      Hegel was an exponent of 'the synthetic method'? If he did, he
      was mistaken. The *Logic*, talks about both the analytic and
      synthetic methods. In the final section of *The Science of Logic*, the
      Absolute Idea, Hegel tries to show their essential unity.

> The concrete totality which makes the beginning contains as
> such within itself the beginning of the advance and develop-
> ment. ... The absolute method ... does not behave like
> external reflection but takes the determinate element from its
> own subject matter, since it is itself the subject matter's own
> principle and soul. ... This no less synthetic than analytic
> moment of the *judgement*, by which the universal of the
> beginning of its own accord determines itself out of itself as the
> *other of itself*, is to be named the *dialectical* moment. (p. 831)

36   **28**: 44.
37   **28**: 43.
38   *Introduction to the Critique of Hegel's Philosophy of Law*, **3**: 175–6.
39   *C***1**: 173.
40   Marx to the Editorial Board of *Otechestvenniye Zapiski*, November
      1877.
41   *Ibid*.
42   Preface to *Introduction to the Critique of Political Philosophy*, **29**: 263.
43   *Ibid*.
44   *German Ideology*, **5**: 46. See also **5**: 78.

Appendix
   1   *PR*, para. 289.
   2   *Phen*: 16.
   3   *Phen*: 12.
   4   *Phen*: 10.
   5   *HP*: 17.
   6   *Ibid*.
   7   *SL*: 594.
   8   *SL*: 44.
   9   *E*1, para. 11.
  10   *E*1, para. 81.
  11   *HP*: 3.
  12   *Phen*: 141.
  13   *SL*: 154–5.
  14   *E*1, para. 95, Remark.

15 *E2*, para. 247, Remark.
16 *E2*, para. 248.
17 *E3*, para. 381, Remark.
18 See, for example, *E2*, para. 249, Remark and para. 339, Remark.
19 *PR*, para. 95.
20 See *E1*, para. 173.
21 *Ibid.* See also *SL*: 642.
22 *PR*, para. 185.
23 *PR*, para. 244 and Remark.
24 *C1*, 'Afterword' to the second edition.
25 **1**: 491.
26 **1**: 85.
27 **3**: 63.
28 **3**: 18–19.
29 **3**: 187.
30 **5**: 5.
31 *C3*: 959.
32 **3**: 212–13.
33 **28**: 38.
34 *C3*: 956. See also letter Marx to Engels, 27 June 1867.
35 *C3*: 311.
36 **3**: 217.
37 *Ibid.*
38 *C1*: 169.
39 Books like *The Logic of Marx's Capital*, by Tony Smith (Albany,
    NY: State University of New York Press, 1990) and *Dialectics and
    Social Theory*, by Ali Shamsavari (Braunton, Devon: Merlin,
    1990), typify a type of learned discourse about Marx and Hegel
    which deletes all distinguishing marks between their methods, or
    distinguishes them only by vague references to 'idealism' and
    'materialism'. Such writers never bother to ask themselves *why*
    Hegel's dialectic takes the shape it does. Nor do they consider
    what, if anything, Marx's method has to do with his communism,
    which, by the way, is never so much as mentioned.
40 *PR*, para. 299.
41 Hiroshi Uchida, *Marx's 'Grundrisse' and Hegel's 'Logic'*, (London
    and New York: Routledge, 1988) gives an important exposition
    of this and related ideas. See also, Patrick Murray, *Marx's Theory
    of Scientific Knowledge* (New York: Humanities Press, 1988).
42 **5**: 5.
43 *C1*: 493.

44   *C*1: 494.
45   **3**: 303–4.

5   Some Questions for the Twenty-first Century

1   *Communist Manifesto*, **6**: 506.
2   *C*3: 596.
3   *Critique of Hegel's Philosophy of the State*, Introduction, **3**: 182.
4   *C*1: 925–6.
5   I cannot resist the urge to report here the Three Principles of Democratic Centralism, as formulated by my friend Don Cuckson: 1 Father knows best; 2 Not in front of the children; 3 Keep it in the family.
6   *C*1: 283.

Index